PROVIDING SUPPORTIVE SERVICES TO THE FRAIL ELDERLY IN FEDERALLY ASSISTED HOUSING

URBAN INSTITUTE REPORT 89–2

Raymond J. Struyk, Douglas B. Page, Sandra Newman, Marcia Carroll, Makiko Ueno, Barbara Cohen, and Paul Wright

 THE URBAN INSTITUTE PRESS

Washington, D.C.

June 1989

THE URBAN INSTITUTE PRESS
2100 M Street, N.W.
Washington, D.C. 20037

Library of Congress Cataloging in Publication Data
Providing Supportive Services to the Frail Elderly in Federally
Assisted Housing.
1. Aged--Services for--United States. 2. Aged--Home Care-
-United States. 3. Aged--Government policy--United States.
I. Struyk, Raymond J. II. Series.
(Urban Institute Reports; 89-2, ISSN 0897-7399)
HV1465.P76   362.6'3   89-5796

ISBN 0-87766-462-5
ISBN 0-87766-470-6 (casebound)

Printed in the United States of America.

Distributed by
University Press of America
4720 Boston Way   3 Henrietta Street
Lanham, MD 20706   London WC2E 8LU ENGLAND

URBAN INSTITUTE REPORTS are designed to provide rapid dissemination of research and policy findings. Each report contains timely information and is rigorously reviewed to uphold the highest standards of policy research and analysis.

The Urban Institute is a nonprofit policy research and educational organization established in Washington, D.C., in 1968. Its staff investigates the social and economic problems confronting the nation and government policies and programs designed to alleviate such problems. The Institute disseminates significant findings of its research through the publications program of its Press. The Institute has two goals for work in each of its research areas: to help shape thinking about societal problems and efforts to solve them, and to improve government decisions and performance by providing better information and analytic tools.

Through work that ranges from broad conceptual studies to administrative and technical assistance, Institute researchers contribute to the stock of knowledge available to public officials and private individuals and groups concerned with formulating and implementing more efficient and effective government policy.

Conclusions or opinions expressed in Institute publications are those of the authors and do not necessarily reflect the views of other staff members, officers or trustees of the Institute, advisory groups, or any organizations that provide financial support to the Institute.

CONTENTS

TABLES

ABSTRACT

As the population ages, federal and state governments have become more aware of the need to provide supportive services to the frail elderly in assisted housing. Historically there has been a steep step from the minimal supportive services available in assisted housing environments to the extensive and expensive services provided in nursing homes. Government has an interest in actively coordinating more of a continuum of care and service availability.

This study estimates the number of frail elderly in federally assisted housing at significant risk of institutionalization. It then reviews existing state and federal efforts to serve this population and possible new service approaches. It also presents models whereby more states could be encouraged to become involved in serving their own frail elderly populations, and makes recommendations on how best to structure and fund such programs.

ACKNOWLEDGMENT

This report was prepared under contract to the Office of Policy Development and Research, U.S. Department of Housing and Urban Development, in response to a congressional mandate.

EXECUTIVE SUMMARY

Federal and state governments have become more aware of the aging of assisted housing residents and the increasing inability of many to continue to live independently. The provision of housing alone becomes inadequate for elderly whose frailty has increased, and they begin to require assistance with basic activities of daily living. Historically, there has been a steep step between levels of care: from the minimal supportive services typically available in assisted housing environments to the intensive--and expensive--level of care provided by nursing homes. The sharp differences in levels of care offered have meant that some elderly continue to live in independent apartments well beyond their ability to care for themselves and their apartments adequately; others enter nursing homes without genuinely requiring the intensive medical and supervisory care that is provided there.

Government has an interest in actively coordinating and providing more of a continuum of care and service availability, especially in assisted housing environments, for three reasons. First, the support service needs of frail assisted housing residents have gone well beyond the resources and experience that housing managers have for meeting them. The greater burdens placed on the housing managers have prompted a search for solutions. Second, to the extent that some elderly are placed in nursing homes without really needing the full, costly level of support provided there, public monies could be more effectively spent in providing only the necessary level of assistance in a noninstitutional setting. Third, aside from administrative and efficiency rationales for expanding home and community based services, government may decide that it has a desire and/or responsibility to help make up the existing supportive service deficit for its low-income, frail elderly citizens.

Although the first two arguments are gaining strength, they have not yet been sufficiently urgent or well documented to prompt extensive government involvement in supportive service provision for the population of frail elderly in assisted housing. But the potential for improvement in these two areas, combined with the desire to meet the needs of this vulnerable population, has led the federal government and several states to explore supportive service programs. Active states do not attempt to justify their programs on the narrow basis of cost-effectiveness alone; they stress the commitment to alternatives for their elderly citizens to live independently.

This study addresses, in turn, estimates of the number of frail elderly in assisted housing at significant risk of institutionalization, existing state and federal efforts to serve this population, and possible new service approaches. It also presents models whereby more states could be encouraged to become involved in serving their own frail populations and recommendations on how best to structure and fund such programs.

THE FRAIL POPULATION

With data from the National Long Term Care Survey, the Annual Housing Survey, and the Department of Housing and Urban Development (HUD), it is estimated that roughly 105,000 residents of assisted housing over the age of 65 are in need of assistance with at least one activity of daily living, or about 7 percent of all over-65 residents of assisted housing. This number is larger than the number who will actually require institutionalization within the next year or two, but it is less than the one-third of those elderly assisted housing residents who have some degree of frailty. Still, the 105,000 figure is an identifiable group that can be considered at risk of institutionalization and on whom a service program could reasonably expect to target its services. A key finding, thus, is that the population needing assistance is not overwhelmingly large either in total or on a state-by-state basis. This population is expected to grow, however, with the rising share of the elderly over age 75; it would likely rise further if more support services were funded, attracting frail persons to housing projects offering them.

PROVIDING SUPPORTIVE SERVICES

Although many states are recognizing the need for congregate housing, only a few have ventured very far in responding to it. Three models or levels of involvement can be identified:

✦ States fund a statewide service coordinator who directs housing managers to available service resources--no new services or housing are created (Minnesota and Connecticut).

✦ States provide tax-exempt bond financing for the construction of congregate housing facilities--developers are responsible for providing supportive services under loose guidelines, and the states are not involved in service provision or subsidy (Arkansas, Idaho, Illinois, Pennsylvania, North Carolina, Ohio, and Oregon).

✦ States directly provide and/or subsidize the provision of new supportive services to frail elderly in existing senior housing or newly constructed congregate facilities (Connecticut, Maine, Maryland, Massachusetts, New Jersey, New Hampshire, New York, Vermont, and Oregon).

This third model is clearly the most appropriate for frail residents of existing assisted rental housing, people who require more support services than are currently available in place and who would not be able to pay for them without government assistance. The nine state supportive service programs fitting this third model are compared, and four--Massachusetts, Maryland, New York, and Oregon--are described in detail.

After an examination of the experiences of state programs, the Farmers Home Administration/Administration on Aging National Demonstration of Congregate Housing for the Elderly in Rural Areas (basically a Model II program at the federal level), and the HUD Congregate Housing Services Program (essentially a Model III program at the federal level), the key elements in an effective system of delivering supportive services to the frail elderly in assisted housing can be identified.

First, in selecting the elderly to receive supportive services, those evaluating prospective participants must be trained and given clear guidance on the degree of impairment that constitutes sufficient severity to warrant admission. A key point in this area is the great need for more research to define accurate predictors of risk of institutionalization and corresponding assessment tools for local use. Given current knowledge, a reasonable standard that could be implemented consistently is the presence of at least one activity of daily living limitation severe enough to require personal assistance and one or more instrumental activity of daily living limitation. Use of a centralized screening system at the local level, rather than staff at each project conducting their own assessments, is preferable because it permits more consistent application of guidelines in a process that inevitably requires judgments to be made. In general, improvements in targeting and screening increase both the likelihood of savings from delayed institutionalization and the willingness of states to participate.

Careful case management and tailoring of services are central to any cost containment effort and to effectively meeting the individual needs of participants. The skills of the on-site coordinator and regular contact with the coordinator, as at mealtimes, are important in this regard. Formal client evaluation and modification of the service package should be repeated at least annually after admission into the program. Moreover, copayments from participants, based on income and on the quantity of services received, are advisable; both offset program costs and help contain service use.

A core package of nonmedical services should be offered at each facility, but mandatory participation in a service is justifiable only when economies of scale in its provision outweigh tailoring considerations, as may be so with congregate meal service. A higher level of services (including medical services) than can be offered by congregate programs could be arranged through state Medicaid offices using waivered home and community-based service options.

In terms of tailoring and avoidance of overservicing, there are strong arguments for providing cash payments to housing providers with which to purchase services from vendors or to deliver them directly, rather than forcing projects to broker in-kind services from several sources that are funded directly by a variety of state agencies. Unifying the sources of funds to the provider into a single payment would simplify management and coordination tasks. In the case of federally assisted housing, channeling the funds through a single federal agency is appropriate. These changes would leave coordinators freer to fit services specifically to client needs and to provide needed services themselves, where appropriate, or to purchase them from vendors offering a less expensive quality product.

Further, agency oversight would be essential for ensuring the quality and adequacy of services. Thorough supervision may necessitate cooperation between the federal agency's area offices and state social service agencies. Such oversight becomes particularly important when housing projects have greater responsibility for service provision under the "cash budget" arrangement outlined. Oversight would be facilitated by channeling funds to a project through HUD rather than another agency, because HUD would then have firm information on each project's resources. On the other hand, social service agencies have areas of expertise that HUD lacks.

Although programs currently operating could be--and in many cases are being--modified to be consistent with the lessons learned from experience to date, most have a substantial distance to go. Several possible new approaches show promise for serving frail elderly residents of assisted housing. They include the Housing and Support Services Certificate Program, social/health maintenance organizations, and the Congregate Housing Certificate Program.

Under the Housing Support Services Certificate Program (HSSCP), frail elders determined by the administering agent (the local housing authority or a nonprofit organization, possibly including a current sponsor in the Section 202 program) to be eligible would receive a certificate covering the costs of support services. The payments for services would be used by the local administering agent to provide case management and the necessary support services, either directly or through various vendors. In principle, the agent could contract out the whole case management and service delivery responsibility; it could also contract with several vendors and allow households to select among them. HSSCP has yet to be implemented.

Four social/health maintenance organizations (S/HMOs) have been in operation on a demonstration basis since 1985. Under this model, a single private provider organization assumes responsibility for a full range of ambulatory, acute inpatient, nursing home, home health, and personal care services under a prospectively determined fixed budget. All elderly residents of assisted housing in a locality would be encouraged to enroll in an S/HMO that would then be wholly responsible for case management, tailoring, and provision of services to clients. The residents' monthly capitated enrollment fees would be subsidized in whole or in part.

Under the Congregate Housing Certificate Program (CHCP), which exists only in concept, households eligible on the basis of low income and high risk of institutionalization would receive a certificate entitling them to occupy a unit in a congregate housing project that provides independent living with the necessary nonmedical support services. The voucher would cover the cost of both housing and the level of support services warranted, with the households contributing 50-60 percent of their incomes toward the combined costs. As proposed, vouchers could be used at approved privately operated facilities.

These options represent several of many that could be developed from basic building blocks designed to improve targeting, control costs, and improve tailoring of services to match needs. The amount of responsibility assigned to agencies versus that given to individual elderly persons for securing services, the extent of integration of payments for housing and support services, and the application of and approach to existing housing programs could all be varied. The models presented are good examples of what could be done.

These promising options should be further developed and evaluated. Now is an appropriate time for experimentation among these options in light of the growing population of frail elderly and the uncertainty about how best to proceed. To this end, four recommendations are made:

✦ If Congress continues funding for the Congregate Housing Services Program (CHSP)[1] as a laboratory for analyzing the effects of program improvements, the CHSP should be altered to conform with the "best practices" outlined above. Moreover, it seems reasonable that if a joint state-federal financing model is adopted for providing assistance to additional households, it should be applied to CHSP as well.

✦ Demonstrate the Housing and Support Services Certificate Program in several cities for 5-10 years. This approach holds great promise for assisting frail elders in units assisted with Section 8 and housing vouchers and for those living in housing projects. The discipline of providing services within the resources provided by the certificate may achieve substantial efficiencies.

Considerable latitude should be given to participating local administering agencies in the early years in the ways they elect to deliver services (e.g., subcontracting for the entire program, alternative arrangements with state and local social service agencies); based on experience, superior alternatives should be identified.

✦ Active, intense experimentation with capitated programs should be continued. HUD, working with the Health Care Financing Administration, should enroll all the elderly in assisted housing in a community in an S/HMO for a demonstration period of 5-10 years. This would provide an excellent test of acceptance by assisted housing occupants and the efficacy of the incentives in capitated systems for achieving better tailoring and case management, which should lead to lower costs and greater delays in institutionalization. The best candidate S/HMO may be the Kaiser Permanente program in Portland, Oregon. (Residents in existing congregate projects might be excluded, in part to use these projects as a control group.)

✦ Demonstrate the Congregate Housing Certificate model in a couple cities to evaluate its cost containment and service responsiveness attributes that should come from the cost limits imposed by the Augmented Fair

Market Rents and competition among projects. The demonstration would have to involve enough projects to make competition meaningful and would have to be staged for a long enough time (7-10 years) to induce private housing suppliers to participate. Although CHCP may be of limited use in serving the current population of frail elders in assisted housing, it is recommended for a demonstration on the basis of what may be learned for future program design.

More analysis of the possibilities of the Supplemental Security Income supplements for funding supportive services in assisted housing also appears warranted in light of New York's successful use of this model. In several respects, including cost limits, it resembles CHCP.

The recommendations call for relatively long demonstration periods, from 5 to 10 years. In part, they are needed to induce private suppliers to participate. At least as important, however, the long demonstration period provides the opportunity for an initial evaluation, program adjustment, and subsequent evaluation (i.e., the possiblity of measuring improvements made in program performance based on early findings).

FUNDING THE SERVICES

Both state and federal governments have an interest in providing for vulnerable elderly citizens. Both have experimented with congregate housing programs. Both have traditionally shared the responsibility for providing health and welfare services, and both would share in the savings from reduced institutional costs that accrue from providing more support services to elderly in assisted housing. Hence, models of joint federal-state funding and cooperation are appropriate. In brief, any program must ensure that all states have an incentive to participate and mobilize the necessary resources. But although the federal government can provide incentives and leadership, it is the responsibility of the states to choose whether and in what form to participate.

Three such models of joint federal-state cooperation are explored:

1. the federal government's contributing certain forms of housing assistance and states' contributing the supportive services to the frail elderly occupying these units;

2. federal-state funding of supportive services from the savings in Medicaid expenditures that may accrue from delayed institutionalization of the frail elderly (there is considerable uncertainty about the existence and magnitude of these savings); and

3. independent of a possible linkage created through Medicaid savings, federal-state funding of services for federal- and state-assisted housing units occupied by frail elderly persons.

Over the next few years, the third option has the most to recommend it, in large part because of the lack of essential information about the others, such as the likely savings to Medicaid associated with more efficient congregate housing programs and the realistic range of parameters for the first model (i.e., federal housing/state services). Although the state programs evolved under option three would share certain standard elements--such as targeting and tailoring requirements--which federal agencies would have strong hand in designing, there is also room for, and indeed a need for, state participation in the design and implementation of service programs.

Calculations show that, nationally, it would cost between $441 million and $819 million annually to serve the estimated 105,000 over-65 residents in assisted housing who need assistance with one or more activity of daily living. Any program or combination of programs could be expected to substitute in part for some other governmental spending (e.g., Medicaid, Medicare) and to redirect or use some existing related funds (e.g., Title III, Social Services Block Grants) so that the net additional costs would be considerably less.

Moreover, some system of tenant copayments and federal-state matching would also serve to distribute the burden more fairly among recipients, states, and the federal government. Of course, the population of frail elderly with limitation in at least one activity of daily living (ADL) in assisted housing can be expected to increase in the years ahead. We estimate growth by some 35,000 by the year 2000, under simple assumptions. The costs quoted above (and throughout the report) would rise proportionately, if all these additional persons received support services.

Analysis of state expenditures on related services with funds from the Social Services Block Grant program and Title III of the Older Americans Act shows that state contributions to a new program could be funded from those sources, if the states elected to do so, without severely affecting other activities. Of course, the value to the states of the other services now being provided should not be underestimated. The federal share of the total cost after tenant copayments--perhaps 50-60 percent of the total--would be new appropriations. As noted, however, much of this may be offset by savings elsewhere.

In short, the costs and the population to be served are not prohibitively large. Based on current experience and the further analysis provided in this report, however, it is difficult to endorse any single approach to delivering the services at this time. Instead, as noted, the coming years are an important time for frank experimentation and refinement for the country to learn to deal with its growing population of increasingly frail elderly at a reasonable cost to the rest of society.

Note, executive summary

1.   The Reagan administration's Fiscal Year 1990 budget recommends halting funding for CHSP.

INTRODUCTION

Currently, about 1.76 million households headed by a person aged 62 or over are estimated to live in housing whose cost to the occupant has been reduced through federal subsidies (Department of Housing and Urban Development, Office of Policy Development and Research). This number is likely to grow as the share of the elderly in the total population increases with the aging of the baby boom generation. The U.S. population over age 65 that numbered 28.6 million in 1985 will, in 2010, total about 39 million, or 14 percent of the population. In the same year, 19 million will be 75 or older and 6.5 million will be older than 85 (Struyk, Turner, and Ueno, 1988, figure 2.1 and table A.1).

This aging of the population, which is also occurring in the assisted housing stock, underlies the congressional mandate for the present study. Because the prevalence of functional limitations increases as a population ages, so does the need for a range of supportive services--such needs as assistance with personal care like dressing or bathing or with household tasks like cooking and cleaning (National Center for Health Statistics 1987). Yet there is reason to believe that many people have service needs that are not being met. According to the 1984 National Health Interview Survey, for example, about 30 percent of all noninstitutionalized persons 65 and older needing help dressing, 40 percent needing help bathing, and 44 percent needing help getting outside reported that they did not receive help with these activities (NCHS 1987). In addition, a 1986 study of 100 large public housing authorities (PHAs), representing about 200,000 elderly-headed households, addresses service gaps in one subgroup of assisted housing (Holshauser 1988; Newman 1986). First, the demographic characteristics of residents suggest the need for supportive services: about three-fourths of these elderly public housing residents live alone, more than one-third are 75 or older, and more than 4 in 10 have lived in the same location for at least 15 years, with the likelihood that their environments have become increasingly unsuitable to their needs over time. Second, despite the efforts to link frail elderly tenants to a wide array of services, including case management, homemaker/home health aide services, and transportation, more than three-fourths of PHAs reported that they are faced with tenant requests for services that they are incapable of handling.

Although incomplete, this evidence suggests that elderly residents in assisted housing may be increasingly at risk over time because their service needs are not being met. The widening service gap threatens the continued independence of many in this population, the majority of whom are very low income and who, unless they receive help to remain independent, realistically face only one alternative: institutionalization. In many cases, such institutional placement is inappropriate because the individual requires a lower level of assistance than is routinely provided in institutions; in nearly all cases, the elderly would prefer to continue to live in the community with as much independence as possible.

Family members and friends are the primary source of assistance to the frail elderly as a group. This point is also true for the frail elderly living in assisted housing. The vast majority of the elderly in assisted housing live alone, and many now receive some formal services through myriad patchwork systems worked out at the local level using programs funded with federal, state, and local monies. However, these arrangements are fragile with respect to continued funding. They are often inefficient because of the limited tailoring of services to meet the specific needs of the elderly client. Additionally, many housing managers charged with coordinating the provision of services to the frail elderly are not well equipped to make decisions on whom to assist and what help to provide.

This report responds to congressional interest in improving on the existing situation in order to increase the life quality of the frail elderly in assisted housing and to develop a more efficient approach to providing necessary assistance. In particular, Section 163 of the Housing and Community Development Act of 1987 requires that a report be prepared by a private entity with funding and guidance from the Department of Housing and Urban Development (HUD) on the number of frail elderly in federally assisted housing and alternatives for funding and delivering support services. After estimating the number of frail elderly in assisted housing, this report reviews and assesses an array of alternative systems that might be implemented.

In a consideration of alternatives, the diversity of the existing housing assistance and supportive service provision modalities must be kept in mind. Housing assistance models include housing projects built with federal aid that are especially designed for the elderly, similar projects designed for use by a variety of ages (family projects), and rent supplements under the Section 8 certificate and housing voucher programs to households in private housing throughout an area. The delivery of formal supportive services to the frail elderly is equally diverse. Some state programs use direct contracts between local agencies (often using federal funds) and service vendors for a predefined set of services to those identified as eligible to receive them. Others disburse federal, state, or local funds to individual subsidized housing projects to purchase services needed by their frail occupants. Still other projects employ a combination of these two approaches. Individuals who can afford to do so may purchase services from private vendors or sometimes from public agencies. In the future, individuals or governments on behalf of poor individuals living in assisted housing may purchase "insurance" from vendors, such as social health maintenance organizations, to provide the necessary services.

The diversity of current arrangements may suggest that no system works well in all environments. Instead, matching delivery systems to housing circumstances may be in order.

Fortunately, there is a considerable body of experience on which to build an assessment of how improvements might be made. The Congregate Housing Services Program has used funds appropriated to HUD to purchase services for occupants of assisted housing projects especially designed for the elderly.

A similar program has been demonstrated by the Farmers Home Administration. In addition, a number of states have taken bold and creative initiatives in this area. Yet other systems are in the design and experimental stages.[1]

This report concentrates on a few key elements of the various candidate systems for delivering supportive services to the frail elderly in assisted housing. They include the degree to which systems target subsidized services to those elderly who are genuinely at risk of institutionalization, the degree to which the services provided correspond to those most needed by an individual frail elderly person, the cost per month of services provided, and the applicability of a given system in alternative assisted housing environments. Under many systems, a critical additional element is the coordination of services from various sources to individual clients.

Beyond the design of an effective system of assistance, the system must be funded. Although federal and state governments are anxious to improve the lives of the frail elderly, the constrained fiscal context of funding decisions cannot be ignored. The practicality of federal-state cooperation in designing and funding services to the frail elderly is motivated by fiscal realities, the tradition of federal-state support for welfare and health programs (e.g., Medicaid, Aid to Families with Dependent Children), and the experience that both levels of government bring to the design of a new system for providing services in assisted housing. To encompass the range of experience, this report draws on evidence available from state and federal systems for providing services and explores a range of joint funding arrangements.

The balance of the report consists of six chapters. Chapter 2 defines the size and composition of the "at-risk" population of elderly now living in assisted housing. Chapters 3 to 5 describe, respectively, current state congregate housing and other programs providing services to the frail elderly in assisted housing, the types and amounts of existing federal resources for carrying out this task--including the Congregate Housing Services Program and germane social programs--and new approaches to providing these services. Chapter 6 outlines three possible models of federal-state cooperation for providing these services and assesses the ability of the states to participate under current funding arrangements and levels; in principle, all these models are workable in all states. Chapter 7 provides recommendations on both the design of the delivery system and the way to fund it.

Note, chapter 1

1.   Given resource constraints, a comprehensive survey of supportive services currently available in assisted housing is beyond the scope of this effort.

2

THE SIZE AND ATTRIBUTES OF THE FRAIL ELDERLY POPULATION IN ASSISTED HOUSING

Fundamental to the consideration of supportive services to the frail elderly living in government-assisted housing is estimating the size and characteristics of this population. This information is essential for evaluating alternative strategies for meeting the service needs of this population, for assessing the costs of these approaches, and for selecting the target group of recipients.

This chapter addresses the questions of population size and attributes. It first briefly describes data sources, methods, and definitions.

DATA, METHODS, AND DEFINITIONS[1]

No reliable administrative data exist on how many elderly living in assisted housing are frail or at risk of institutionalization. Because a survey of elderly residents in assisted housing was beyond the scope of this study, we used several analytic techniques with data from two large Census surveys: the national Annual Housing Survey (AHS) and the National Long Term Care Survey (LTC). The 1978 AHS, the source of data on the number of frail elderly who live in assisted housing, was used because it included a one-time supplemental block of questions on health and functional status of each household member. Within the AHS, the frail elderly were defined as individuals 65 years of age or older who had either a personal mobility limitation (such as difficulty getting around or negotiating stairs) or at least two health conditions (such as heart problems or serious trouble seeing or hearing).[2]

Residents in assisted housing were identified as those who responded affirmatively to either of the following two questions:

1. "Is this [house/apartment] in a public housing project, that is, is it owned by a local housing authority or other local public agency?"
2. "Are you paying a lower rent because the Federal, State, or local government is paying part of the cost?"

The LTC, in which the same sample was interviewed in both 1982 and 1984, was the source of estimates on the specific nature of the frailties that characterize the elderly and on the size and attributes of the at-risk population. The LTC was administered to a nationally representative sample of 6,190 frail individuals 65 and older.[3] Because the LTC followed the 1982 sample members who were institutionalized by 1984, it provides a direct measure of at-risk status--namely, whether an individual entered a nursing home within the following two years. The LTC is also a rich source of information on functional status, including limitations in ADL, impairments in IADL, and cognitive impairments. The presence of a cognitive impairment is measured by a short series of mental status questions administered to all respondents.

Because the estimates of people 65 and older living in assisted housing, on the one hand, and the estimates of functional limitations and at-risk status, on the other, are derived from different data sources, the two data sets were linked. This task involved identifying a subsample of AHS individuals 65 and older who are matched on a number of characteristics to the LTC sample (i.e., the frail elderly, as defined above) and then categorizing them by the assisted housing measures available on the AHS. These housing assistance measures were then appended to the LTC by predicting their values in the matched AHS subsample of frail elderly and then applying these predicted values to the LTC. (These procedures are described in detail in Appendix A.)

Before the estimates and characteristics of the population of interest are discussed, several features of the approach are worthy of note:

✦ The four-year time difference between the AHS data (1978) and the LTC data (1982, 1984) should present a problem only in the event that there were systematic changes in the prevalence or characteristics of frail and at-risk elderly who reside in government assisted housing. Although the data necessary to investigate this issue are not available, the age distributions of residents 62 and older in assisted housing in 1978 and 1983 are quite similar. (See Appendix C, table C.8.) Because frailty, at-risk status, and age are correlated, it is likely that a snapshot of the elderly living in assisted housing in 1978 will provide a reasonable approximation of the elderly in 1982 and 1984.

✦ The age of eligibility for special housing assistance for the elderly is age 62. We have adjusted our estimates to reflect the status of those 65 and older because the LTC sample excludes individuals younger than 65. This exclusion implies that the aggregate estimates of the total number of frail elderly in assisted housing provided in this paper are smaller than the "true" size of this population but that the proportions of frail elderly are larger than the "true" proportions because of the lower rates of functional limitations and institutional risk among those 62-64.

✦ All the results given in this chapter pertain to a population broader than those living in federally assisted housing for two reasons. No studies have been done of the measurement error in answers to the two AHS questions on residence in assisted housing. Furthermore, the second question explicitly refers to nonfederal sources of housing assistance.

The extent to which these factors distort the estimates is unknown. The estimates should, however, provide reasonable orders of magnitude.[4]

ESTIMATING THE SIZE AND CHARACTERISTICS OF THE FRAIL ELDERLY POPULATION IN ASSISTED HOUSING

Despite the comprehensiveness of the LTC, neither it nor any other long term care data base can be said to include a standard set of measures of frailty and institutional risk. Although there is general consensus that the dimensions included in the LTC are important indicators of frailty in the elderly, no consensus exists on the best ways to measure these dimensions or their effects on such outcomes as future institutionalization.[5] This lack of agreement was recently highlighted by the National Committee on Vital and Health Statistics Subcommittee on Long-Term Care (1988). The subcommittee identified 11 issues in functional status measurement that remain unresolved, including such fundamental questions as whether differences in capacity versus differences in performance should be ascertained and how data collection methods (e.g., self-reports, patient records, knowledgeable sources) affect prevalence rates.

The absence of standard measures of frailty and risk has two implications for this report. First, all the estimates provided here must be viewed as approximations of the underlying characteristics that are of interest, namely, frailty and institutional risk. Second, selecting a single measure of frailty or impairment on which to base either estimates of eligible participants in a supportive services program or program costs has no particular methodological justification. Instead, we have based this decision on more practical criteria: first, that the measure is potentially simple and efficient to collect either through self-report, observation, or professional assessments and second, that it distinguishes a target population frail enough to be in some jeopardy of not being capable of continued independent living but not so frail as to need intensive monitoring and services that are generally beyond the abilities of most noninstitutional settings to provide. This second criterion essentially identifies a window of eligible persons, some of whom are more incapacitated by activity limitations and some who are less impaired, but all of whom are frail.

There is another, broader implication
standard operational measures of frailty: progr
to identify and aid only those genuinely aι .
institutionalization will have difficulty making the
identification. The targeting of services will be correspondingly
loose. However, as discussed in chapter 3, some improvement
in program operations is possible even with existing knowledge.

As noted later, the measure of impairment adopted in the ✓
remaining chapters of this report is the presence of at least one
limitation in an ADL such that the frail person requires
personal assistance. Somewhere between 75,000 and 135,000
occupants 65 and older of assisted housing meet this criterion.
The purpose of this chapter, however, is to explore various
measures of frailty and risk.

As implied earlier, there are numerous ways to define the
subgroup of elderly in assisted housing who might be
considered the most appropriate target for a supportive
services program. The broadest definition includes those who
require assistance to carry out daily activities, often referred to
as the frail elderly. As shown in table 2.1, about 24 percent
people of people 65 and older living in assisted housing meet
this broad definition of frailty.[6] Applying this fraction to the
1.52 million elderly households estimated to live in assisted
housing in 1987 by the Department of Housing and Urban
Development, Office of Policy Development and Research
results in an approximation of 365,000 households with some
frailty.[7] Table 2.1 also indicates that the rate of frailty in
assisted housing (at the midpoints of the ranges) is about 6.2
percentage points higher than that for elderly persons who do
not live in assisted housing.

A more specific sense of the institutional risk and
impairment characteristics of these frail elderly is given in table
2.2. The table provides information on three factors: (a)
institutional risk, measured by a two-year experience in two
ways: first, as any instance of institutionalization, regardless
of duration or placement on a nursing home waiting list, and
second, as permanent institutionalization measured as 90 days
or more; (b) functional limitations, measured in four ways:
first, as a count of the number of activities of daily living
(including transfer, mobility, dressing, bathing, toileting, and

TABLE 2.1   ESTIMATED PROPORTIONS OF THE FRAIL ELDERLY
LIVING IN, AND OUT OF, GOVERNMENT-ASSISTED
HOUSING (Renters Only)

	In Assisted Housing	Not In Assisted Housing
Proportion with some frailty[a]	19.8% - 28.2%[b]	16.2% - 19.4%[b]
Unweighted case counts	144	578

Source: 1978 National American Housing Survey.

a. "Some frailty" is defined as having at least two of 20 medical conditions
(e.g., heart trouble, arthritis) or one of five difficulties with personal mobility
(e.g., getting around outside, going up or down stairs).

b. The range represents the 95 percent confidence interval around the
estimated proportion. (See Appendix B.)

eating) that require the assistance of another person to carry
out; second, as needing personal assistance with any of six
ADLs (transfer, mobility, dressing, bathing, toileting, and
eating); third, as needing personal assistance with eating or
toileting (the two ADLs that indicate a more serious level of
impairment); and fourth, the need for personal assistance with
any of nine IADLs (heavy housework, light housework, laundry,
preparing meals, shopping for groceries, getting around
outside, going places beyond walking distance, managing
money, and making phone calls); and (c) cognitive impairment,
measured by the mental status question set mentioned earlier.
     The first column indicates that about 18 percent of the
frail elderly in assisted housing (about 66,000 persons) are

TABLE 2.2   INSTITUTIONAL RISK AND FUNCTIONAL IMPAIR-
MENTS OF THE FRAIL LIVING IN, AND OUT OF,
GOVERNMENT-ASSISTED HOUSING (Renters Only)

	Proportions of Frail Elderly Renters	
Institutional risk	In Assisted Housing	Not in Assisted Housing
Institutionalized within 2 years or on nursing home waiting list	12.2-23.2[a]	16.0-21.8[a]
Institutionalized within 2 years for 90 days or more	3.3-10.9	8.0-12.6
Functional limitations		
Needs assistance with		
1 ADL[b]	11.9- 22.9	15.0-20.8
2 ADLs	1.5-7.7	5.1-8.9
3 or more ADLs	2.9-10.1	16.3-22.3
Needs assistance with at least 1 ADL	22.0-35.4	40.2-47.6
Needs assistance with either eating or toileting	3.3-10.9	11.1-16.3
Needs assistance with at least 1 IADL[c]	94.6-99.4	97.6-99.4
Cognitive Impairment[d]		
Yes	21.1-34.1	24.6-31.2
Unweighted case counts	268	1021

Source: Linked 1978 AHS and 1982-84 National Long-Term Care Surveys.
a. Each range represents the 95 percent confidence interval around the
estimated proportion. (See Appendix B.)
b. ADLs are activities of daily living that include: transferring, mobility,
dressing, bathing, toileting, and eating.
c. IDALs are instrumental activities of daily living include: heavy
housework, light housework, laundry, preparing meals, shopping for
groceries, getting around outside, going places beyond walking distance,
managing money, and making telephone calls.
d. Sample individuals were considered to have cognitive impairments if they
scored below average (for the LTC sample as a whole) on a standardized test
of cognitive impairment, the Short Portable Mental Status Quiz.

are likely either to become institutionalized or to put their names on a nursing waiting list within two years, and about 8 percent (29,000) are likely to become permanently institutionalized. These rates of institutional risk are not significantly different from those for the frail elderly who do not live in assisted housing.

The rates of cognitive impairment and IADL needs also do not differ significantly for these two groups; roughly 28 percent of the frail elderly, regardless of housing assistance, are found to be cognitively impaired, and nearly all (97-99 percent) need assistance with some IADL.

In contrast, compared with those not in assisted housing there appears to be a much smaller prevalence of ADL needs among the frail elderly living in assisted housing: about 6 percent report three or more ADL needs, about 28 percent report any ADL need, and roughly 7 percent report need for assistance with eating or toileting. These rates differ sharply for other frail elderly: 19 percent for three or more ADLs, 44 percent for any ADL, and 14 percent for eating or toileting.

Why would two groups who are about equally likely to be at risk of institutionalization have such different ADL characteristics? One interpretation may be that because the frail elderly with ADL limitations--and, particularly, the most demanding needs like eating or toileting--are difficult to serve in assisted housing as it now exists, they are the elderly tenants who are asked to leave or for whom nursing home placements are made. In fact, the institutional risk rates of assisted housing tenants are similar, even though a smaller fraction of these frail tenants have the serious kinds of needs for which nursing homes may be appropriate. This point suggests that other characteristics not based on impairments place them at risk.

Some insight into these risk factors is provided in table 2.3. Three entries in this table are of particular interest. First, the frail elderly in assisted housing are considerably more likely to live alone than their counterparts living elsewhere. The absence of someone else in the dwelling to help with everything from routine tasks to a life-threatening emergency may reasonably be viewed as a risk factor. Second, informal, unpaid caregivers--friends or relatives, for example--are less likely to be available to the frail elderly in assisted housing to fill the gap associated with living alone. Although there is a greater prevalence of formal, paid caregivers among the frail elderly in assisted housing, neither the nature of the services provided by these paid assistants nor the suitability of the match between services and client needs is known. Furthermore, the ability to sustain these arrangements over time is questionable[8]. In addition, the frail elderly in assisted housing have very low incomes, severely limiting their alternatives to nursing home placement.

Beyond describing the impairments and institutional risk characteristics of the frail elderly, the three sets of attributes displayed in table 2.2 can also serve as alternative ways to identify the target population for a supportive service strategy in assisted housing. The prevalence rates produced by these definitions are shown in table 2.4. The table indicates, for example, that if the presence of at least one ADL need were adopted as the criterion for eligibility, between 4.9 and 8.9 percent of all elderly tenants in assisted housing (or between about 75,000 and 135,000 persons) would qualify. Alternatively, if the selection criterion were the presence of one or more IADL need, this fraction would increase to 23 percent (or between about 293,000 and 415,000 persons). Further, if the more restrictive standard of three or more ADL needs were used, the proportion would drop to between 0.4 and 2.8 percent (roughly between 6,000 and 43,000).

Because a primary goal of introducing supportive services into assisted housing is to postpone or prevent institutionalization, the two institutional risk groups, by definition, would represent the sharpest or most efficient targeting. Roughly 4 percent of elderly tenants fall into the more liberally defined risk group (about 61,000 persons); about 1.7 percent fall into the more restrictive group of the permanently institutionalized (about 26,000 persons). The rates shown in the table are based on longitudinal data capturing two years of actual experience.

TABLE 2.3   CHARACTERISTICS OF THE FRAIL ELDERLY
LIVING IN ASSISTED HOUSING (Renters Only),
1982 (Weighted Percentage)

	In Assisted Housing	Not in Assisted Housing
Sex		
Male	16.0	33.0
Female	84.0	67.1
Age		
65-69	27.0	19.3
70-74	28.6	19.8
75-79	18.0	21.9
80-84	14.9	20.0
85-89	10.2	12.5
90 or older	1.4	6.6
Race		
White	68.1	87.8
Nonwhite	31.9	12.2
Household Composition		
Male living alone	8.8	8.5
Female living alone	65.3	37.5
Couple	17.5	32.1
Living with others	8.5	22.0
Education		
High school graduate	30.7	29.7
Not high school graduate	69.3	70.3
Medicaid Eligibility		
Yes	45.1	34.4
No	54.9	65.6
Availability of support		
Any unpaid helpers		
Yes	75.0	85.2
No	25.0	14.8

	In Assisted Housing	Not in Assisted Housing
Any paid helpers		
Yes	40.1	29.8
No	60.0	70.2
Income (1982)		
$<3,000	40.8	21.0
3,000-4,999	41.3	32.5
5,000-6,999	16.8	17.4
2,000-8,999	0.8	12.6
9,000-9,999	0.3	2.7
10,000 or more	0	13.7
Region		
Northeast	31.9	24.8
North Central	35.9	19.0
South	18.8	36.6
West	13.5	19.6
Metropolitan status		
In SMSA	71.5	50.9
Outside SMSA	28.5	49.1
Number of stories		
<4	26.3	12.0
4 or more	73.7	88.0
Gross Rent (1982)		
$<100	51.6	40.2
100-149	24.7	13.4
150-199	8.3	10.4
200-249	6.3	11.2
250-299	4.5	7.4
300-349	1.5	5.8
350-399	1.0	4.5
400 or More	1.7	7.1
Unweighted case counts	268	1021

Source: Linked 1978 AHS and 1982-84 National Long-Term Care Surveys.

TABLE 2.4   INSTITUTIONAL RISK AND FUNCTIONAL
            IMPAIRMENTS OF ALL THE ELDERLY LIVING
            IN, AND OUT OF,GOVERNMENT-ASSISTED
            HOUSING (Renters Only)

| | Proportions of All Elderly Renters | |
Institutional risk	In Assisted Housing	Not in Assisted Housing
Institutional risk		
Institutionalized within 2 years or on nursing home waiting List	2.7-5.7[a]	2.8-4.0[a]
Institutionalized within 2 years for 90 days or more	0 .7-2.7	1.4-2.2
Functional Limitations		
Needs assistance with		
1 ADL[b]	2.2-6.0	2.4-3.8
2 ADLs	0.1-2.1	0.7- 1.7
3 or more ADLs	0.4-2.8	2.7- 4.0
Needs assistance with at least 1 ADL	4.9-8.9	6.8-8.8
Needs assistance with either eating or toileting	0 .7-2.7	1.9-2.9
Needs assistance with at least 1 IADL[c]	19.3-27.3	16.0-19.0
III. Cognitive Impairment[d]		
Yes	4.7-8.5	4.3-5.7
Unweighted case counts	599	3250

Source: Linked 1978 AHS and 1982-84 National Long-Term Care Surveys.

Note: Because the LTC includes only frail elderly sample members, the total number of elderly was derived by applying the ratio of the frail elderly to the total elderly in the AHS. In particular, we assumed that the nonfrail elderly in the AHS did not have any of the functional impairment or institutional risk characteristics being estimated. Using this assumption, we solved for the weighted number of all elderly in the LTC (designated "X") as follows:

$$\frac{\text{frail elderly (AHS)}}{\text{all elderly (AHS)}} = \frac{\text{frail elderly (LTC)}}{X}$$

a. Each range represents the 95 percent confidence interval around the estimated proportion. (See Appendix B.)

b. ADLs are activities of daily living that include: transferring, mobility, dressing, bathing, toileting, and eating.

c. IDALs are instrumental activities of daily living that include: heavy housework, light housework, laundry, preparing meals, shopping for groceries, getting around outside, going places beyond walking distance, managing money, and making telephone calls.

d. Sample individuals were considered to have cognitive impairments if they scored below average (for the LTC sample as a whole) on a standardized test of cognitive impairment, the Short Portable Mental Status Quiz.

Unfortunately, in contrast to ADL, IADL, and cognitive impairment definitions, for which standard assessment tools exist that could be used to determine tenant eligibility, no measure exists for assessing risk of future institutionalization directly. Table 2.5 provides a rough sense of the degree to which impairments could serve as proxies for risk of institutionalization and highlights a basic problem inherent in this approach. For example, only about one-third of the institutional risk groups have an ADL impairment, which requires them to have assistance. Therefore, need for assistance with ADLs, which can be measured, is an imprecise substitute for actual risk status.

A program designed to preempt institutionalization must serve those whom it identifies to be potentially at risk, and this targeting can be as good only as the best available functional assessment procedure. As discussed earlier, none of the available measures is a good predictor of eventual institutionalization. ADL measures seem to be the best on the combined grounds of practicality and power; they do help identify which elderly renters in assisted housing have one or more ADL limitations that require assistance to offset. Based on this definition, there are between 75,000 and 135,000 households with at least one frail member; the midpoint of the estimate is 105,000. We take this number as a reasonable approximation of those potentially at risk.

TABLE 2.5   FUNCTIONAL IMPAIRMENT CHARACTERISTICS OF
THE FRAIL ELDERLY AT RISK OF INSTITUTION-
ALIZATION LIVING IN GOVERNMENT-ASSISTED
HOUSING (Percentage of Risk Group with Given Impairments)

	Institutionalized within 2 Years or on Nursing Home Waiting List	Institutionalized within 2 Years for 90 Days or More
Functional limitations		
Needs assistance with at least 1 ADL[a]	33.1	34.3
Needs assistance with either eating or toileting	6.0	3.6
Needs assistance with at least 1 IADL[b]	100.0	100.0
Cognitive Impairment		
Yes	28.1	35.6
Unweighted case counts	47	19

Source: Linked 1978 AHS and 1982-84 National Long-Term Care Surveys.
Note: Because of the small sample sizes, these figures should be taken as
illustrative.
a. ADLs are activities of daily living that include: transferring, mobility,
dressing, bathing, toileting, and eating.
b. IDALs are instrumental activities of daily living that include: heavy
housework, light housework, laundry, preparing meals, shopping for
groceries, getting around outside, going places beyond walking distance,
managing money, and making telephone calls.
c. Sample individuals were considered to have cognitive impairments if they
scored below average (for the LTC sample as a whole) on a standardized test
of cognitive impairment, the Short Portable Mental Status Quiz.

Notes, chapter 2

1.   These issues are discussed more completely in Appendix A. Genevieve Kenney provided valuable assistance in the tasks described in Appendices A and B.

2.   Note that terms ("frail," "at-risk," etc.) defined specifically in this chapter and its associated Appendices A, B, and C are sometimes used in a more general way throughout the rest of the study.

3.   The sampling frame was a list of 36,000 names from the Health Insurance Master File (i.e., Medicare beneficiaries). Eligible sample members were those with some frailty defined as having, or expecting to have, a problem for three months or longer with any activity of daily living (ADL) (i.e., eating, getting in or out of bed, getting in or out of chairs, mobility inside, mobility outside, dressing, bathing, getting to or using the toilet, incontinence of bladder or bowel), or instrumental activity of daily living (IADL) (i.e., preparing meals, doing laundry, light housework, grocery shopping, managing money, taking medicine, making phone calls). Screening was done either in person or by phone. Although 6,393 cases were screened into the sample, 508 of them were determined to be "false positives" (e.g., when the ADL or IADL need no longer existed at the time of the interview), and another 203 cases were no longer available for interviewing at the time of the survey (mainly due to death). We dropped the false positive cases from our analysis file, yielding an initial analysis sample of 5,580 (U.S. Department of Health and Human Services, undated; and Manton and Liu, 1987).

4.   Personal communication with Duane McGough, Division of Housing and Demographic Analysis, Department of Housing and Urban Development, Office of Policy Development and Research, May 26, 1988.

5.   Two significant sources documenting the importance of these domains are: U.S. Department of Health, Education, and Welfare (1979) and National Institutes of Health (1987).

6.   The 24 percent estimate is the midpoint of the confidence interval shown in the table. This interval represents the margin of error associated with the point estimate. (See Appendix B.)

7.   Note that the 24 percent prevalence rate is based on persons, whereas the 1987 count is based on households. The prevalence of multiperson frailty among households in assisted housing is quite low. (See Appendix A.) Nevertheless, the application of person rates to households produces slight underestimates.

8.   In particular, this is a very low income group, and even under subsidy programs, there may be copayments, deductibles, or other program rules that limit the duration and intensity of services.

3

STATE INTEGRATED HOUSING/SERVICE PROGRAMS

This chapter examines various state programs developed to meet the supportive service needs of the frail elderly who require assistance to maintain independent living. Special emphasis is given to states that have instituted an integrated housing/services program for residents of public or assisted housing. Within this group, particularly interesting state programs are selected for closer program reviews. (Appendix D contains a case study of each of the states that were studied more closely.) Several specific program aspects are reviewed. They include eligibility criteria by which the program identifies frail elders who need support services and the extent to which each program tailors services to the needs of individual participants. The reviews are followed by a discussion of the mechanisms for coordinating service delivery within programs and the degree of coordination among state agencies. The chapter ends with discussions of the cost to the state of subsidizing program participants, the use or nonuse of copayments by program participants, and evaluations of the programs.[1]

INFORMATION USED AND MODEL TYPOLOGY

Information on state programs came from available literature, telephone interviews, and in some cases visits to the state agencies. When we relied on the literature, including state regulations, we cannot be as specific about some program aspects as we would like. When 1987 cost figures were unavailable, we have inflated the latest available figures to 1987 dollars.

Many states have recognized the need for providing support services, and state programs providing assistance for independent living can be usefully divided into three models, summarized in table 3.1.

Model I

This program is a statewide mechanism whereby a state housing finance agency funds a social service resource person to help housing managers identify and find solutions for nonshelter problems of elderly tenants. No direct subsidy of services is involved. Training sessions and technical assistance are provided to housing managers to spot potential health and social problems that could lead managers to terminate older tenants' leases.

Minnesota's Housing Finance Agency (MHFA), for example, funds one human service coordinator for MHFA-financed housing projects. The objective of the program is help older tenants who need supportive services to remain independent gain access to existing service agencies. The human service coordinator surveys social and health agencies across communities and provides this information to housing owners, managers, and elderly tenants. Training sessions and technical assistance are arranged for owners and managers on working with elderly tenants, families, and local service providers to ensure that needed supportive services are provided.

In addition, MHFA requires that, during the underwriting process, prospective owners describe how the housing projects will respond to support service needs of elderly tenants. The human service coordinator then works with owners to help them recognize the needs of older tenants and find solutions to their problems.

TABLE 3.1   STATE INITIATIVES IN PROVIDING SERVICES TO
THE FRAIL ELDERLY LIVING IN GOVERNMENT-
ASSISTED HOUSING

Model I

A statewide human service coordinator position is created to provide technical assistance and resource information to managers of subsidized housing with elderly tenants. Local health and social service resources are surveyed, and training is provided for managers and prospective developers on supportive service needs of elderly tenants. No new services are created.

States: Minnesota   Connecticut

Model II

Housing finance agencies provide tax-exempt bond financing for the construction of congregate housing facilities. Twenty percent of the units are reserved for low-income elderly tenants. Developers are responsible for providing supportive services.

States: Arkansas   Idaho
                 Illinois   Pennsylvania
                 North Carolina   Ohio
                 Oregon   Connecticut

Model III

The state subsidizes a program of supportive services for the frail elderly. Services are provided to a set number of elderly in existing senior housing buildings or newly constructed congregate facilities. A specified core set of services is provided, typically including congregate meals, personal care, social services, housekeeping, transportation, and laundry.

States: Connecticut   New Hampshire
                 Maine   New York
                 Maryland   Vermont
                 Massachusetts   Oregon
                 New Jersey

Model II

Several state housing finance agencies (HFAs) have financed the construction of private congregate housing facilities through tax-exempt issues; some use Department of Housing and Urban Development/Federal Housing Administration (HUD/FHA) 221(d)(4) mortgage insurance.[2] Federal law requires that when tax-exempt bonds or low-income tax credits are used, a proportion of the units must be set aside for low-income elderly: at least 20 percent for those at or below 50 percent of the area median income or 40 percent for those at or below 60 percent of the area median income. The subsidy goes only to units serving income-eligible households. There is no state subsidy or coordination involved in providing supportive services. The HFAs usually set a minimum age requirement and in most cases mandate that one meal a day be provided to residents.

Ohio's Housing Finance Agency (OHFA) is a good example. OHFA has provided tax-exempt bond financing for the construction of 19 congregate facilities since 1983. Nonprofit and for-profit entities are eligible to participate in the program. The service package typically includes one mandatory meal a day, transportation, weekly housecleaning, laundry services, and social services. All units are fully private apartments, and the facilities have congregate dining rooms.

OHFA has no authority to enforce rent ceilings, but it suggests that rents be between 30 percent and 80 percent of the area median income. OHFA reports that rents range from $800 to $1,200 a month, with an additional service charge between $250 and $400 a month. All services are arranged by the housing manager. There is no formal coordination mechanism between OHFA's congregate financing program and the state's unit on aging or other state service agencies.

Model III

The focal point in this model is a state-funded congregate housing service program that adopts a comprehensive scheme to regulate the services for the frail elderly and provides a subsidy to pay for supportive services to eligible program participants. Although state programs falling within this category pursue a variety of approaches, they share features in a number of key areas:

✦ The programs limit the availability of services to elderly who are frail. Most states define frail as someone who requires help with at least one ADL. The exceptions are Massachusettts and New Jersey, where elderly who are physically independent but socially isolated may participate in the program.

✦ Program participants pay a sliding fee for supportive services. Participants are primarily low- and moderate-income persons who receive a subsidy, but private-pay participants with no subsidy are generally not excluded.

✦ Both multifamily buildings and single-family homes are employed in the programs. The majority of multifamily housing is public housing or subsidized housing facilities, although some are fully private, nonassisted housing.

✦ Program participants in multifamily buildings generally have their own individual apartments, and participants in single-family homes have private bedrooms. Massachusetts uses shared apartments and shared homes with private bedrooms.

✦ Each program is administered by a state agency or agencies with extensive regulatory authority. The state agency controls the type of services provided, the fees charged, and the subsidy provided.

✦ Services are planned and organized and delivered on a project-by-project basis. For each project, there is a project sponsor who has developed and obtained approval for a specific service/subsidy plan and is responsible for overseeing the provision of services. There is some flexibility in developing a service plan to tailor it to the particular needs of the program's participants.

✦ Project sponsors are generally limited to nonprofit groups, local housing authorities, and other public agencies.

✦ A number of states limit the percentage of residents in a multifamily building that may participate in the program. The rationale for these ceilings is to avoid creation of an institutionalized atmosphere.

✦ Most states require that existing funding streams or in-kind services be tapped prior to using state congregate program funds.

✦ Considerable variety typically exists in the funding sources used to provide subsidies.

The states in this category include Connecticut, Maine, Maryland, Massachusetts, New Hampshire, New Jersey, New York, Oregon, and Vermont. From this list of states, we selected Maryland, New York, Massachusetts, and Oregon for closer examination of their state-funded congregate programs. Table 3.2 summarizes key aspects of state programs in this category. In general, the programs are quite small, often representing informal demonstrations rather than major state programs. The balance of this chapter focuses on key aspects of the Model III programs because the primary concern of this report is with approaches that integrate the delivery of housing assistance and services.

ELIGIBILITY CRITERIA

Eligibility criteria for state-funded congregate housing programs generally limit access to applicants who need some assistance in performing the daily activities of living while screening out applicants whose physical and behavioral limitations are such as to require constant supervision. From here, the eligibility criteria and the manner in which they are applied diverge widely in the various states.

Apart from physical criteria, most state-funded congregate programs do limit entry to adults who are over 60 years old.

Data from several state programs indicate, however, that the average age is significantly higher than the minimum requirement. For example, the average age of a New York Enriched Housing participant is 83 years old; the average age for a Maryland Multifamily Enriched Housing participant is 81; the median age for a Massachusetts congregate public housing participant is 77.

Some state-funded congregate programs are targeted to public and assisted housing and therefore include primarily low- and moderate-income participants. For example, the Massachusetts program is part of its state-funded elderly senior public housing program, and eligible applicants must first be income eligible for state public housing. Other state programs are limited to elders who are income eligible for other forms of assistance. New Jersey requires that eligible participants have discretionary incomes of less than 126 percent of the Office of Management and Budget poverty level. However, most state congregate programs do not set additional program-specific income eligibility requirements for admission.

The most common admission standard--applied in Maryland, New York, Maine, Vermont, and Oregon--is that an applicant must be functionally impaired in regard to at least one activity of daily living (ADL). For example, Maryland eligibility regulations require that applicants have a physical or mental condition that inhibits the performance of one or more ADL. New Hampshire requires impairment in performing three or more ADLs. But there is as yet no standard definition or measurement procedure across the states for determining ADL impairment or assistance needs. Massachusetts and New Jersey, by contrast, extend eligibility to applicants who may not need formal support services but desire to live in a congregate housing environment in order to avoid social isolation. State admission criteria usually articulate the general concept that applicants should not require extensive nursing or hospital care--a level of care not provided in a congregate housing setting--and often identify general characteristics that would exclude an applicant from eligibility.

TABLE 3.2   SUMMARY OF STATE CONGREGATE HOUSING PROGRAMS

STATES	New York	Maryland	Massachusetts	Oregon
Year began	1978	1976	1978	1984
Overview of Program	Program avail to up to 25% of residents in existing public and assisted housing	Program avail to up to 25% of res in existing pub & assisted housing and private group homes	State-financed specially designed congregate units in conventional sen public housing as well as 100% cong facilities.	Prog in 3 newly constructed elder bldgs, 20% of 1 bldg for Medicaid
Oversight	Dept of Social Serv	Department on Aging	Communities & Devel, Elder Affrs	Sen Serv Div
License	Licensed	Certified	Certified	Licensed
# Facilities	44	35 Multifamily, 65 Homes	39	3
# Residents	500 (est)	1,000 Multifam, 548 Homes	397 Residents in Occupancy	300
Description of Units	Fully private apts, a few shared units	Multifam bldg with private apts, group homes with priv bedrooms	Shared apts & shared homes with private bedrooms	Fully private apts
Sponsors	Nonprofit groups or public agencies	Housing auth, nonprofit groups	Human Service Agencies, Housing Authorities	For-profit/non-profit devel
Eligibility	65+ w/ADL impair, no continuous nursing, no income eligibility, but est 75% are SSI eligible	62+ w/ADL imapirment, no income eligibility, but majority of multi-family projects in assisted housing	62+ w/ADL impairment or socially isolated, no constant superv or max assistance with ADLS, income eligibility for public housing, likelihood to remain 1 year	No min age, avg age 87, ADL impair, need 24-hr supervision
Services	Standard[a], 1 required meal/7 days	Standard[a], 3 required meal/7 Days	Standard[a], + health aides, no required meal	Standard[a], medical assistance, 3 meals

a.   Standard services include congregate meal, housekeeping, personal care, laundry, transportation, and social services.

STATES	New York	Maryland	Massachusetts	Oregon
Year began	1978	1976	1978	1984
Service Delivery	Own staff, contracted meals (own staff)	Own staff, contracted title 5 senior aides, meals (Title 3C), own staff, contracted	Own staff, home care corp, visiting nurse, meals (Title 3), own staff, contracted	Own staff contracted
Staff	Coordinator, personal care, housekeepers, cook	Coordinator, pers care, housekeeping, var meal staff	Coordinator, var meal staff, personal care contracted with home care corp	Coordinator, personal care
State's Annual Cost	$1.5M	Multifam: $1.25M, group homes: $620,000	$66M govt. obligation bond issued 1987, $144M home care program	NA
State's Monthly Sub	$350 per person ($435 cap)	$125 per person ($500 cap for grp homes)	$795 per person	$275 per assisted person
Money Flow	State supplements SSI checks, participants pay sponsor, state funds start-up and project deficits	Dept of Aging pays sponsors through AAAS	EOCD funds Housing Auth for construc/rennov of cong facil and housing operating expenses, Elder Affairs funds coordinators' salary and services	State pays part of Medicaid costs facilities financed by state housing fin agency
Source of Subsidy	State SSI supplement	General funds	State bonds, general funds, Medicaid	State's 2176 Medicaid waiver funds
Participant Copayment	Sliding scale	Sliding scale	Sliding scale	Maj fully private paying
Observation	$5 deficit/person/day experienced by 22 of 24 project sponsors	State considering elim 3 meal req, also has demonstration cong project with 24 hour supervision	Reliance on existing service providers, MOU at state and local levels for coordinated service delivery	Medically oriented program

b. NA = not available.

TABLE 3.2 (continued)

STATES	Vermont	Maine	Connecticut	New Jersey	New Hampshire
Year began	1979	1984	1977	1981	1987
Overview of Program	Program avail to residents in public and senior housing, no cap	Prog avail to up to 15-20% of res in senior public housing	State financed spec designed cong facilities	Up to 25% of res in pub senior housing	Demon project avail to 25-30% of res in pub senior housing
Oversight	Office on Aging	Bureau of Elderly	Department of Housing	Dept on Aging	Dept of Soc Serv
License	Not required	Licensed	Certified	Not required	Certified
# Facilities	18	16	5	37	1
# Residents	102	147	168	750 (est)	30
Description of units	Fully private apts	Fully private apts	Fully private apts	Fully private apts	Fully private apts
Sponsors	AAAs	AAAs with local housing authority	Local housing auth, nonprofit housing corp	Nonprofit, housing auth	Housing authority
Eligibility	60+, ADL impairment, no income eligibility	60+, ADL impair no income elig	62+, ADL impaired, income eligibility for public housing	62+ with ADL impair/socially isolated, income elig of <126% of OMB pov level	No min age, avg age 74, 3 ADL impairments, no income elig
Services	Standard[a], no required meal	Standard[a], 1 req meal/7days	Standard[a],24hr superv 1 req meal/7 days	Standard[a], 1 req meal/7days	Standard[a], 2 req meals/7 days

a. Standard services include congregate meal, housekeeping, personal care, laundry, transportation, and social services.

STATES	Vermont	Maine	Connecticut	New Jersey	New Hampshire
Year began	1979	1984	1977	1981	1987
Service Delivery	Own staff, contracted meals (Title 3), staff, contracted	Own staff, contract meals (Title 3), staff, contracted	Own staff, contracted meals (own staff), contracted	Own staff, contracted meals (own staff, contract, Title 3)	Own staff, contracted meals (own staff)
Staff	AAA staff	Shared care mgr, part-time staff	Coordinator, personal care, housekeeping, var meal staff	Coordinator, var staff	Coordinator, contracted meal staff
State's Annual Cost	$90,000	$301,275	$33M state bond issued ($5.6M spent)	$1.8M	$120,000
State's Monthly Sub.	$80 per person ($100 cap)	$186 per person	NA[b]	NA[b] (no cap)	$333/person
Money Flow	Office on Aging pays AAAs	Bureau on Aging pays AAAs	Dept of Housing fin construct/renov of facil, Dept on Aging subsidizes services	Aging dept pays sponsor + portion of coordinator salary	State pays housing authority
Source of Subsidy	General funds	General funds	State bonds, general funds	Casino rev	General funds
Participant copayment	No required copayment, vol contributions	Sliding scale	Sliding scale	Sliding scale	sliding scale
Observation	No state program regulations, instructions to AAAs developed by Office on Aging	State evaluation of program completed late 1988		Cong residents can work up to 20 hrs/wk	State targeting nursing home residents for cong partic

b. NA = not available.

Two characteristics of the more common admission criteria deserve comment. First, these programs focus on a frail elderly population that encompasses persons with significantly different service need levels. These service need levels range from modest to so extensive as to be just short of constant supervision. Second, the decision as to whether an applicant falls within the boundary of eligibility (i.e., whether the level of impairment is sufficient to require assistance but not so severe as to require constant supervision) often involves a discretionary judgment that is difficult to make.

The manner in which discretionary eligibility criteria are implemented, and the service level needs of program participants that result, have obvious policy implications. Most important is the policy issue of whether the program seeks a participant population with mixed service need levels or one with more uniformity in the service need level--and, if the latter, whether a high or low average level of need is sought. This policy decision is perhaps just as important for an individual congregate facility as for the statewide program. On the other hand, a mix of need levels within a congregate project encourages interactive support among participants, avoids an institutional atmosphere (a predominance of severely frail residents), and moderates the aging-in-place phenomenon. Still, there may be operating efficiencies in providing services on a relatively standardized basis, which would argue in favor of a more consistent needs level in the population served. Moreover, to the extent that a program involves a subsidy, a state may prefer to target the subsidy to persons at the higher end of the needs spectrum. This choice would argue in favor of a high needs level. Further, to the extent that higher service levels are more likely to enable people at risk of institutionalization to avoid it, the potential saving could be greater for narrowly targeted programs.

The Maryland Sheltered Housing program is a good example of a relatively discretionary set of admission criteria. To be eligible for admission, an applicant must be physically or mentally impaired, defined as a "condition which inhibits a person's ability to perform one or more of the activities of daily living." This requirement is amplified by the additional requirement that an applicant needs assistance with the activities of daily living, such as meals and housekeeping. In addition, Sheltered Housing sets an upper limit on assistance needs by requiring an applicant to be "able to function" in the congregate setting. Taken as a whole, these criteria can be interpreted to mean that an applicant must need assistance with one ADL in order to qualify for the program.

Admission criteria such as Maryland's are so general that applying them to individual applicants requires considerable discretionary judgment. Admission decisions are further complicated by the fact that it may be difficult to judge an applicant's capabilities, assistance needs, and behavior patterns based on information gathered in an interview.

Some states (Massachusetts, New Jersey, and Maine) use Professional Assessment Committees (PACs) to determine applicant eligibility in accordance with state regulations. PAC membership generally consists of representatives of social service and health agencies, mental health clinics, and senior citizen groups to provide professional input in the decision-making process. Generally a congregate housing coordinator will conduct the actual screening of applicants and make admission recommendations to the PAC for a final admission decision.

The admission interview is key in determining whether an applicant should be admitted to a congregate program. Maryland, New York, and Massachusetts report that admission interviews are conducted without applicant family members present to eliminate the prospect of relatives answering interview questions instead of the applicant, and applicants giving guarded answers. Massachusetts congregate guidelines require two personal interview sessions, with one of the interviews conducted at the applicant's home, to assist in determining an applicant's suitability for the congregate program.

New York, Massachusetts, Oregon, and Maryland have separately developed their own standardized functional assessment tools to guide congregate housing coordinators in conducting an admission interview and to provide a framework for making an admission decision. Maryland's Sheltered Housing functional assessment tool is a detailed set of interview questions divided into six functional areas: physical health, mental health, memory, physical maintenance, ADL, and IADL. (ADLs and IADLs are listed in table 2.2, notes b and c.) The coordinator is directed to rate the applicant in each functional area using a five-point scale. The structure of the questionnaire and the accompanying instructions reinforce the more general admission standard that applicants in need of constant medical or nursing supervision, as well as those who do not require assistance in any activity of daily living, are to be rejected. Even so, the Maryland assessment questionnaire does not eliminate the need for the coordinator to exercise considerable discretion in judging whether an applicant's service needs are beyond Sheltered Housing's service capability--or conversely, whether assistance is required at all.

New York's Enriched Housing program is more vague than the Maryland program in defining the minimum assistance needs required to qualify for admission, but it is more specific in indicating disabilities or behavior characteristics that warrant exclusion. To qualify for New York Enriched Housing, the regulations merely state that an applicant must "require the services" offered by the program. But the regulations enumerate 16 characteristics that require exclusion. These characteristics can be grouped as: the need for continual medical or nursing supervision, serious mental disability, physical immobility (bedfast), or behavior that would interfere with the operation of the program.

The admission criteria for the Massachusetts program differ significantly from those of Maryland, New York, and most other states in regard to the minimum level of assistance need that is required for admission. As noted, eligibility is extended not just to those who are functionally impaired and need assistance with activities of daily living but also to those who have "an emotional or social need for a group living environment."

Typically, the admission criteria in state congregate program statutes and regulations are general. This characteristic gives project coordinators broad discretion in interpreting the rules and applying them to individual applicants. The fact that many important admission criteria, such as behavior traits or assistance needs, are difficult to assess during an interview further magnifies the discretionary nature of the admission decisions that must be made by project coordinators.

SERVICE TAILORING

Supportive services are generally provided on an as-needed basis, although there are several cases of packages of services being prescribed and in a few programs some services are mandated for all program participants. Congregate housing projects generally provide the following supportive services: a congregate meal, housekeeping, personal care, laundry services, transportation, and social services. The level of use of services by each participant is determined by the initial needs assessment and periodic reevaluations. In state programs that require a PAC for each congregate project, each service package is reviewed by the PAC for its adequacy in meeting the participants' service needs.

New York requires that coordinators conduct a formal reevaluation of participant service needs each year. Most states conduct some periodic reevaluation on an as-needed basis, but practices and frequency vary widely. Maryland, New York, and Massachusetts report that congregate coordinators keep "incident reports" on each participant. These reports describe any significant incidents involving participants that may "red flag" potential health or emotional problems. Congregate coordinators in these states report that the congregate mealtime is a good opportunity for coordinators to spot any behavior or health problems among participants that may require a review of the service needs of the participant.

The degree to which services are tailored to each participant's needs is influenced by the funding and coordination mechanisms for supportive services. For example, under New York's Enriched Housing program, supportive services are funded through an additional state supplement to participants' monthly Supplemental Security Income (SSI) checks. This supplement, which is set by the state legislature, authorizes project sponsors to charge a fixed service fee for each participant. This fee, in turn, provides an incentive to the sponsors to do somewhat more tailoring to keep costs within allowed limits. Similarly, under Maryland's Sheltered Housing program, each multifamily facility must work within a $150 maximum subsidy per participant that the state provides to subsidize service needs.

If agency control of service fees is too restrictive, however, congregate facilities may find themselves operating with a deficit. In fact, New York service costs have risen faster than the legislatively authorized service fee, to the extent that 22 of the 24 Enriched Housing sponsors have program deficits requiring additional state funds to meet operating costs. Yet when site coordinators are not subject to dollar cost limits but instead broker services from state-funded service vendors, the coordinators may broker more services for their clients than are strictly needed simply because they are available. Since services are limited other sites are short changed. Conversely, the absence of cash payments makes it difficult to procure services not already available from state-funded sources to assisted housing residents restricted largely to their buildings, leading to the danger of inappropriate tailoring of services.

In summary, program subsidy levels and congregate housing coordinator skills influence the degree of service tailoring to participant needs. Although we have no precise information to judge the effectiveness of service tailoring, observations from five congregate site visits in four states conducted for this report reveal that coordinators spent a great deal of time with participants at the admission stage to determine participants' initial service needs. Further, most congregate programs rely on occasional reviews of participants' needs and service packages triggered by demonstrated behavior and physical changes of participants. Again, the skill of the coordinator is crucial in recognizing subtle changes that may require an adjustment in the level of services required by participants.

COORDINATION MECHANISM

A key ingredient for a successful congregate housing program is an effective mechanism to coordinate the provision of supportive services to congregate participants. At one end of the spectrum, the majority of states using Model III strategies rely on individual project sponsors to assume the responsibility for coordinating the provision of supportive services to congregate participants.

Maryland is a good example. The Maryland Office on Aging provides technical assistance to congregate sponsors in identifying service providers to tap for their individual congregate projects. However, it is the responsibility of the individual sponsor, and especially the site coordinator, to ensure that adequate services are delivered to congregate participants.

At the other end of the coordination spectrum is the formalized working agreement between appropriate state agencies to ensure that congregate participants receive services that are made available by a variety of state and local agencies. Massachusetts is an example of this model. Under the Massachusetts program, an interagency agreement entered into by the state's public housing, aging, and public welfare agencies spells out each agency's role and level of commitment to the congregate housing program. A key understanding in the interagency agreement is that congregate housing participants have priority status for the state-funded home care program, which provides the bulk of formal supportive services required by congregate participants. Additionally, the home care program has established a more lenient income eligibility standard for congregate participants than for the elderly population at large.

Many congregate facilities make use of existing in-kind services, such as homemaker services or home-delivered meals, which are sometimes available in many communities through the commendable efforts of local service agencies and the funding provided by federal, state, and charitable organizations. These services are often important in meeting the needs of frail elderly citizens, and in some sense it would seem to make sense to build on them, filling in with a new program only the gaps remaining in service offerings in a particular area. In fact, some states do precisely this, either leaving it to individual project sponsors to uncover and arrange for whatever services are already available or, as in Massachusetts, becoming involved at a state level in coordinating service provision for congregate facilities from a variety of agencies.

Unfortunately, this patchwork approach seldom meets all the needs of frail elders in assisted housing. First, the RANGE of support services available is unlikely to provide all the support that a frail elder requires to continue living independently. Second, existing funding constraints on such service agencies mean that much need (in terms of the NUMBER of elders that can be served) goes unmet; some states give residents of congregate projects priority for services that protects them from this problem. Third, this approach typically fails to take advantage of the economies of SCALE and LOCATION that naturally occur in apartment settings, where many residents needing assistance are concentrated in close proximity.

And further, the approach contains several structural INEFFICIENCIES that are relevant to this study. They arise largely from the incentives for tailoring discussed earlier. Where in-kind services are available at little or no additional cost to the project, there may be little incentive to conserve on these services. A service coordinator--who, understandably, is often something of an advocate for the clients in the facility--may arrange for as many of these services as possible, regardless of specific client needs, simply because they are available. Although these incremental services come at little or no cost to the project, they are ultimately drawing down the sources of funds for supportive services in less than efficient ways. On the other hand, coordinators may be unable to procure key services that would genuinely facilitate independent living and for which there is demonstrable need. For these reasons, programs that are given a cash budget with which to purchase appropriate services for each client are more likely to be able to meet client needs reliably and at lower costs.

Existing agencies could still serve as vendors, and indeed their experience is invaluable.

The linchpin in coordinating supportive services, wherever on the coordination spectrum a program lies, is the congregate housing coordinator. The coordinator is generally hired by the project sponsor, with his or her salary paid partially or fully by the state. Major responsibilities of the coordinator include screening prospective applicants, complying with various program reporting requirements, preparing operating budgets, overseeing the delivery of supportive services to program participants, assisting participants in adjusting to congregate living, and performing case management.

Some states mandate that a specific amount of the coordinator's time be set aside for individual case management. New York requires that coordinators spend one-half hour per week per participant on case management. There is some concern on the part of state agencies that an inordinate amount of the coordinators' time is spent brokering services from a variety of sources, leaving insufficient time for actual case management. Although this situation may be a significant problem, coordinators reported during site visits conducted for this report that they have sufficient time to spend with participants.

With respect to credentials, Massachusetts and New York require that the coordinator have a master's degree in social work or a bachelor's degree with several years experience working with the elderly. Maryland has not established specific professional requirements, but each coordinator must complete a state certification program conducted by the state's Office on Aging. New Jersey does not mandate any specific coordinator job qualifications, and some project coordinators have been elevated from congregate home care aides. The New Jersey approach is to rely on the expertise of project sponsors to select coordinators who are proficient in working with elders and dealing with a myriad of social service and health agencies.[3]

Regardless of the academic credentials of coordinators, it is evident from the range of state experiences that the coordinator has a direct and significant impact on the success of a program and on the daily life of congregate participants--from the initial application to termination of residency. On the basis of these experiences, it seems essential that some qualifications for coordinators be established. Areas to be considered in defining requirements include: experience in working with elders, ability to understand and implement assessment questionnaires, familiarity with social and health service agencies in the community, ability to work with other service providers, and willingness to promote the congregate program to the community.

COSTS

It is difficult to compare the costs of providing services under the various state congregate housing programs. This difficulty arises in part because of basic differences in program structures that make cost comparisons unwieldy and in part because some state programs do not have detailed cost data readily available.

There are also accounting inconsistencies. Some state programs include rent as well as supportive services in calculating average cost per participant, for example. In states where congregate services are provided or arranged by a variety of congregate sponsors, the average cost per participant cannot be computed directly from agency budgets, but only from consolidated budget data from all congregate projects. And a statewide average cost may be relatively uninformative because the cost of congregate services also varies significantly among congregate projects within the same program.

Thus a strong caveat must be attached to the comparative costs discussed in this section. In addition to the difficulties already mentioned, in some states, certain program costs may have been overlooked because they were assigned to collateral budgets that were not included in the cost calculations. More generally, different levels of efficiency or cost control ability cannot be directly inferred from the differences in average monthly costs because there may be significant differences in the scope and quality of services provided under the various state programs. At this time, there is no systematic analysis of causes of the variation in supportive services among state-sponsored projects. Nevertheless, the cost figures compared here provide some insight into the orders of magnitude involved.

The total revenue (total fees) collected by a congregate project sponsor for providing services--including all state and federal subsidies and all participant contributions--is generally the same as the total cost of the services because sponsors operate on a nonprofit basis. Thus, as a general rule, the average fee per participant at a congregate project--inclusive of subsidies and participant contributions--is equal to the average cost of congregate services.

The Maryland Sheltered Housing program is representative of state programs in which a variety of project sponsors provide supportive services and the sponsors have some flexibility in setting fees for congregate services. The Maryland Office on Aging estimates that the average monthly cost (i.e., average monthly fee) for the program as a whole is approximately $300 per participant. The Urban Institute examined the budgets of two Maryland congregate facilities and found that their average monthly costs for services were $329 and $367.

The Maryland program imposes no explicit ceiling on monthly fees, but a number of constraints indirectly limit the monthly fee. First, the project sponsor must specify the monthly fee proposed for each participant, and this fee is subject to prior approval from the Maryland Office on Aging.

Second, at least in multifamily facilities, the vast majority of participants are lower-income elders with little income available for service fees. In fact, most multifamily facilities are public housing, assisted housing projects, or private apartment buildings sponsored by a nonprofit organization with a commitment to servicing lower-income people. Third, virtually all participants in multifamily facilities require a state subsidy to pay the monthly fee; thus the Office on Aging is in a position to limit the monthly fee indirectly by controlling the amount of the subsidy.

The single congregate facility in New Hampshire, a public housing project for seniors, has an average monthly cost for services of $469 per participant. That this service cost structure is slightly higher than Maryland's is not surprising, given that the New Hampshire program consists of only one demonstration facility with substantial administrative costs.

The three congregate facilities in the Oregon program provide more extensive medical care than most other congregate programs. The monthly cost for services for participants receiving the lowest level of congregate services (i.e., the service level most comparable to other state congregate programs) ranges from $450 to $540 per month.

The New York Enriched Housing program is significantly different from the other state programs in that the New York legislature has established a direct price control over the monthly fee (cost) structure. Under the New York program, the monthly fee is fixed for all participants at a rate equal to the statutory Congregate Care Level II SSI rate minus a relatively uniform personal allowance for each participant. Given the current SSI Level II rate of $789 (downstate) and $759 (upstate) and a personal allowance that averages $100, the monthly fee under the New York program is approximately $689 or $659, again depending on location. However, it is important to distinguish this monthly fee from the average monthly fee (cost) for services discussed in the other programs above because the New York fee covers rent and utilities as well as supportive services. Further, enriched housing projects actually spend more on housing and services than the Level II supplement allows for; through "deficit financing," the state helps to offset this overrun, which averages $150 per person annually.

In Massachusetts, where congregate facilities are exclusively senior public housing and congregate services are primarily delivered through a state-administered home care program, the average direct service cost is $280 plus $192 for a project coordinator's salary.

SUBSIDY AND PARTICIPANT COPAYMENT

The majority of participants in congregate housing programs receive a subsidy to cover a portion of the cost of the monthly service fee. In New York, approximately 75 percent of all

Enriched Housing participants receive a subsidy. Maryland indicates that a significant percentage of its group home projects are private pay but private pay participants are not common in the multifamily facilities. In Massachusetts, where all facilities are assisted housing, all participants are subsidized by definition. As always, however, there are exceptions; Oregon, for example, reports that less than 10 percent of program participants receive subsidies.

Subsidized participants are generally required to pay a portion of the monthly service fee (a copayment) out of their own income. As a general matter, the subsidy provided is equal to the monthly service fee less the participant's available income. Thus, unless the participant's available income is larger than the monthly fee--in which case, no subsidy is provided--the participant will have to pay all of his or her available income to the program. Available income is generally calculated by allowing the participant to deduct from gross monthly income a fixed personal allowance, certain medical expenses, and rent (if not included within the monthly service fee).

In Maryland, to be eligible for a subsidy, a participant's annual income must not be higher than 60 percent of the state's median income. The Maryland congregate program uses a different method for determining subsidy amounts and participants' contributions, depending on whether the facility is a multifamily or group home. According to the Maryland Office on Aging, sponsors of multifamily facilities, on average, are provided $125 for each program participant. The sponsors of multifamily programs must allocate the total state subsidy received among the different participants, depending on their available incomes. The operating assumption is that every participant is eligible for a subsidy, although in fact there may be a few private-pay participants.

The Maryland Group Home Sheltered Housing program has adopted a more flexible subsidy approach. The program subsidy for group homes covers rent as well as services. The state pays a sliding subsidy to the sponsor, which represents the amount by which the monthly fee (services and rent) exceeds participants' net incomes. Net income represents total income less certain medical expenses and the personal allowance, but rent is not deducted. Most important, the state places a ceiling on the monthly subsidy of $500.

In both the congregate housing and group sheltered housing programs in Maryland, sponsors are prevented from raising monthly fees beyond the point at which they can be covered with the maximum subsidy. From the participant's perspective, there is an incentive to stay out of the program so long as the value of the congregate services provided will be less than the monthly fees he or she must pay the sponsor.

The New York Enriched Housing program provides a subsidy to all low-income participants who are eligible for the state's SSI benefits. An eligible participant receives an SSI supplement that is equal to the legislatively established Congregate Care Level II rate less (1) the available federal SSI payment and (2) the participant's fee. As in Maryland, countable income represents total income less a fixed personal allowance, and a low-income person turns over all countable income to project sponsors.

The monthly fee, subsidy, and participant payment structure of the New York program cover rent as well as congregate services. Similarly, the countable income paid by the participant to the sponsor reflects the participant's contribution to both shelter and service costs. The New York Department of Social Services reports that the average state subsidy per participant is $350 per month. New York has imposed a ceiling on the state subsidy of $435 per month.

FUNDING SOURCES

Stability of funding sources is critical in persuading housing managers to permit the establishment of congregate programs in their buildings. The congregate programs in this category have well-established state funding sources, but most rely on specific annual appropriations. The Maryland, Vermont, and Maine congregate housing programs are funded by appropriations using state general funds. They are annual appropriations, which are not as secure as multiyear appropriations; nor are they as reliable as the funding for entitlement programs. New Hampshire has appropriated funds for a two-year congregate demonstration project. New York's Enriched Housing is funded by an annual appropriation to the state's SSI program. Massachusetts and Connecticut finance construction and renovation of their congregate facilities through state bonds and fund the congregate service components through state general funds. New Jersey's congregate program is funded from investment income earned on the state's casino revenue fund and therefore is more reliable than that of other states.

Many states also employ funds from federal sources, which are typically more reliable. Medicare and Medicaid funds are used for visiting nurse and health services provided in both the Massachusetts and Oregon programs. Title III C-1 nutrition programs, when available, are used by individual congregate projects for their meal component. Some states also use Social Services Block Grants, which are available for homemaker and personal assistance.

Maryland reports that many of its congregate projects make use of Older Americans Act Title V or Green Thumb senior citizen workers to complement congregate projects' staff. Other funding streams include local transportation entitlement programs, food stamps, and other welfare programs.

INCENTIVES FOR COST CONTROL

Most states have termination policies to ensure that participants who are no longer appropriate for the program relocate to more suitable living quarters. Reasons for relocating participants include deterioration of physical or mental capabilities to the point at which the program is no longer able to meet the participant's service needs, improved capabilities that make services unnecessary, persistent drinking or other behavior problems, and refusal to use supportive services. New York, Maryland, and Massachusetts report that termination of congregate resident leases is a delicate procedure that involves repeated meetings with the resident and his or her family to ensure that relocation is not too traumatic for the resident.

Some states report that a number of applicants have used the congregate program as a mechanism to bypass lengthy public housing waiting lists and refused the congregate services once they move into the building. Massachusetts requires that congregate participants commit to remain in the congregate setting for at least one year (barring unexpected illness) to reduce the likelihood of disruptive relocations.

All the states using Model III, except Vermont, require some participant contribution toward the congregate service fee, which is an important ingredient to control service use. Fixed participation fees help discourage unnecessary enrollment, and marginal copayments help discourage unnecessary use of additional services once one is in the program. Vermont has no copayment requirements, but participants are encouraged to contribute what they can toward the program. Most states permit fully private-paying clients to participate.

Other state cost control strategies include providing services on an as-needed basis and screening out applicants who are not appropriate for congregate services. Impressions from five site visits in four states are that the congregate programs do a reasonable job of screening out elders who do not require ADL assistance; that congregate participants are, as noted, significantly older on average than the minimum program age requirement; and that most require some level of personal assistance.

Incentives to control program costs are influenced the most by the subsidy ceilings imposed by most state programs. While forcing congregate projects to keep expenses down, such ceilings may inadvertently encourage congregate sponsors to admit inappropriate participants (i.e., elders with a lower level of need for supportive services) to save money. Although the congregate site visits for this report revealed that congregate participants tended to be physically frail, such cost ceilings still present incentives for sponsors to admit less appropriate elders, thus hampering the potential effectiveness of a program.

EVALUATION

None of the states could provide specific data on delayed institutionalization resulting from the provision of support services. However, several states did provide information concerning the number of congregate participants who were nursing home residents prior to entering the congregate programs. Massachusetts, for example, reports that 11.6 percent of its congregate population moved from nursing homes to congregate facilities. New Hamphsire is consciously targeting inappropriately placed nursing home residents for its congregate housing program. A 1982 evaluation of New York's Enriched Housing program found that 17 percent of Enriched Housing participants came from institutions; the one most frequently mentioned was adult homes. A 1984 evaluation of Maine's congregate housing program reported that 22 percent of program participants had previously lived in nursing homes or boarding houses.

With respect to costs, Massachussetts reports that the average monthly cost of congregate care, including housing ($947), compares favorably to the average Medicaid rate for nursing home care ($1,260), but a direct per-person cost comparison, of course, assumes incorrectly that congregate care would reach only those who would otherwise enter a nursing home. Chapter 6 examines the targeting efficiency necessary for congregate care to begin to realize savings relative to the costs of institutionalization.

Some analysts argue that evaluating congregate housing programs strictly on a cost basis is too narrow a viewpoint and that nonquantifiable benefits must be included. Massachusetts believes that its congregate housing program provides alternative housing for at-risk elders, delays their admission into nursing homes, and substitutes for individual public housing units that would be built in the absence of congregate housing. The state is satisfied that its congregate program provides an environment that supports elders in public housing as they age in place. A 1984 evaluation of the Massachusetts congregate housing program confirms these reports, concluding that the program achieved its stated social goal of offsetting social isolation, promoting independence through interdependence, and providing a viable residential option for at-risk elders. Similarly, a 1982 evaluation of New York's Enriched Housing program found that the majority (68 percent) of program participants reported that they were better off since joining the Enriched Housing program.

SUMMARY

Even absent federal incentives or demonstrable savings on state long-term care expenditures, several states have experimented with providing assistance for independent living. State initiatives to address the needs of the frail elderly in assisted housing can be divided into three models. States are involved in providing new services only under Model III, operating in nine states, and it is programs under this model that are the focus of this chapter. Even under the same model, these nine programs are best characterized by their diversity, but, fortunately, it is this diversity that allows some tentative lessons to be drawn from state experience with supportive housing programs.

To reach those who most need support services, programs need a functional assessment procedure to determine initial eligibility. Most require a demonstrated need for assistance in one or more activities of daily living, but no standard method for quantifying this need or defining ADLs has emerged. Instead, the skills of an on-site service coordinator in assessing applicants are typically at least as important as functional assessment instruments. This person is also critical to individual tailoring of service packages and to monitoring changing client needs, both periodically and based on informal daily observation. Programs must determine an upper bound on the level of care that they are willing to offer, and thus they must develop a mechanism for identifying clients who should be moved on to a higher level of care. Most programs try not to become involved in any but the simplest of medical services, and few have sufficient staff to help an individual who requires supervision beyond that compatible with independent apartment living.

The way a supportive service program is structured also influences its efficiency and success. Although it might seem best to take advantage of the variety of in-kind services available in many communities, possibly filling any gaps with program funds, our research suggests that this patchwork approach is not the most viable model. Service coordinators can spend a disproportionate amount of their time uncovering, applying for, and fulfilling the reporting requirements of the several service providers and funding sources available. There may be significant and unpredictable gaps in the range, frequency, and continuity of these services. Moreover, because they are available to the well-intentioned service coordinator at little or no cost to the project, overuse may result, thus diminishing what funds society is making available for this type of services and redirecting these services away from other segments of the community with a greater need. The coordinator, on the other hand, who has a fixed cash budget for each participant and thus the means to procure precisely the services needed by individual clients, is far more likely to tailor service packages appropriately, limit unnecessary service consumption, and leave existing resources for people elsewhere in the community.

Notes, chapter 3

1.   We have not involved more widely applicable programs which provide support services to elderly persons outside institutions. Consistent with the congressional mandate, our attention is on models integrating housing assistance and support services.

2.   The Robert Wood Johnson Foundation will provide funding for up to 10 HFAs to develop innovative approaches for the provision of supportive services for frail elderly in public and assisted housing. (The program is described in Appendix D of this volume.)

3.   For a profile of site managers of elderly housing projects, see Heumann's (1988) description of Illinois.

4

FEDERAL RESOURCES

This chapter discusses federal options and resources that may be used to foster supportive services for the frail elderly in assisted housing. Included are approaches that could either add services to existing housing or create additional units of elderly housing with services. They may involve programs wholly initiated and funded by the federal government or federal funding streams that could be used to support service programs controlled primarily by the states. These resource alternatives are discussed further in chapter 6 in the context of federal-state cooperation.

FEDERAL SUPPORTIVE SERVICES PROGRAMS

The primary impetus for developing supportive services in assisted housing has come from the agencies responsible for providing such housing. They are not necessarily the most experienced or well-suited agencies for providing or coordinating such social services, however. To date, two federal congregate housing programs have been tested in a demonstration context: (1) the National Demonstration of Congregate Housing for the Elderly in Rural Areas, developed jointly by the Farmers Home Administration (FmHA) and the Administration on Aging (AoA) and (2) the Congregate Housing Services Program (CHSP), developed by the Department of Housing and Urban Development (HUD).

Under the three-year FmHA/AoA demonstration, FmHA financed the construction of 10 multifamily rental housing projects in rural counties and provided rental assistance to the majority of tenants.[1] Between 20 and 35 percent of the units were to be for well elderly and handicapped persons requiring limited supervision and supportive services to help them maintain their independence and improve their quality of life. Typically, AoA demonstration funds paid for a service coordinator who worked with the housing manager to screen clients and arrange for services. A minimum package of services was to be provided at each site, including at least five hot meals per week, social activities, and necessary transportation as well as housekeeping and personal care services for those who needed them. Grantees were required to take maximum advantage of existing service resources in the community and not to duplicate services available through other programs. AoA demonstration funds were intended to support the provision of limited gap-filling services until the end of the demonstration in 1983.

Admissions procedures were not prescribed by the program and they varied by project. Some projects had a housing manager and/or service coordinator evaluate applicants; others used a formal assessment committee and standardized functional assessment form. The result was a loosely targeted program in which only 6 percent of incoming participants had one or more activity of daily living (ADL) limitations, and only 50 percent one or more instrumental activity of daily living (IADL) limitations. Although housing vacancy rates for the larger projects were generally low, housing managers indicated a reluctance to turn down applicants to maintain the program's desired case mix or frailty level. For the demonstration as a whole, the proportion of project residents with two or more functional limitations (loosely defined) was reported at 19 percent, just shy of the lower end of the 20-35 percent range intended.

Subsequent to admission, case management also seems to have been inadequate. An evaluation of the program suggested that "monitoring of the ongoing service needs of frail tenants should be a greater concern in congregate projects--to guard against both overservicing and underservicing." The minimal or nonexistent cost of a participant's seeking additional services may lead him or her to consume more than is reasonably necessary; at the same time, the service coordinator has little incentive to override good will by limiting unnecessary access to costly services. The enhanced case management recommended, however, included primarily "unobtrusive monitoring" and still fell short of formal assessment procedures or changes in the structure of program incentives.

No detailed data are available on the costs of services provided. Services were provided from a variety of sources, including existing (often area agency on aging [AAA] community agencies, contracted service vendors, and on-site staff. Recipient copayments seem to have been the exception rather than the rule. Some sites did charge small fees to cover part of some service costs, but a system of voluntary donations was more common. Although the participants were typically low income, they were paying just 25 percent of their income for rent; the highest additional fees charged for support services did not total more than $50 per month and averaged much less. When such a program is expanded or in the absence of generous demonstration funds, it may be reasonable to ask for a more substantial contribution toward items and services that clients would otherwise purchase outside the program (e.g., meals and transportation).

Participants reported satisfaction, but the evaluation found insufficient evidence to judge the program's success at delaying institutionalization. Undoubtedly the program met other needs in the community, including inexpensive, decent housing suitable for the isolated low-income elderly.

Most of the 10 original projects have continued to offer supportive services since the demonstration ended in 1983, and FmHA continues to finance the construction of private congregate facilities under its rural rental housing program.

HUD's Congregate Housing Services Program (CHSP) provides support services to elderly or handicapped persons living in HUD-financed public housing projects built and managed by local public housing authorities (PHAs) and in Section 202 apartments developed and operated by nonprofit sponsors. The program intended specifically to help prevent premature institutionalization. As such, HUD guidelines called for about 20 percent of building residents to be eligible to receive CHSP services because of their risk of institutionalization. Initial participation rates in CHSP elderly projects among those judged to fit this profile ranged from 10 to 35 percent. The history of the program--which was upgraded from demonstration to permanent status in 1987--has been one of progressively tighter eligibility requirements, however. The operational definition of vulnerability or risk of institutionalization was changed from needing assistance in <u>one</u> ADL (1979-82) to lacking an adequate informal support network and needing assistance in <u>two</u> or more ADLs or IADLs, one of which must be in eating or preparing food (1983-86), to meeting the above criteria plus at least <u>three</u> ADL/IADL limitations (1987-present). In 1986, HUD began requiring most CHSP projects to use one of three widely recognized assessment instruments.[2] HUD does not monitor the application of these indices.

Admissions and ongoing case management are handled by a service coordinator and a volunteer Professional Assessment Committee (PAC), which must include at least one medical and one social service professional. An evaluation of the early years of the program (Sherwood, Morris, and Bernstein 1984) found CHSP projects generally successful at identifying and serving residents needing assistance but less successful at screening out those who did not. Although fully 85 percent of the one-quarter of building residents judged to be vulnerable to institutionalization in fact received support services, an additional 25 percent of the more numerous nonvulnerable population was also served. Thus, for some services (such as meals and chores), fully half of those receiving services did not have a need by any strict definition.

Again, it may be that service coordinators and PACs are well motivated and skilled in some areas but not sufficiently cost conscious or equipped with functional assessment tools reliable enough to allow for tighter targeting and tailoring of services. Success at targeting and tailoring varied substantially among projects, but the study found that smaller buildings and those with higher concentrations of frail residents were more successful. This finding and others relating cost-effectiveness to program size may help overcome apprehension about higher concentrations of frail residents creating an undesirable institutional atmosphere.

The program was shown to improve the morale and life satisfaction of participants. But it was found to have no influence on permanent institutionalization rates. On the other hand, a statistically significant impact on rates of short-term institutional placements of participants and nonparticipants was documented after the program became established. Residents of buildings in which CHSP was implemented were institutionalized at only two-thirds the rate of other elderly renters (Sherwood 1985). Although there is no hard evidence, one can conjecture that the impact of the program on institutionalization may have improved beyond this level because established CHSP sites soon began to admit frailer residents and even to accommodate some who were leaving institutions. It is also possible that the impacts on delaying institutionalization may have increased because of the tighter targeting requirements implemented in 1983 and 1987. Although given the loose guidance on targeting, this point is far from certain.

Meal service was seen as the core of the program, with mandatory 14-meal-per-week service at each site. Most projects also offered housekeeping services, but fewer than half provided personal care, shopping assistance, or transportation services. As with the FmHA/AoA program, projects were required to exhaust existing community service resources before spending CHSP funds on supplementary services. There was a specific maintenance of effort requirement whereby projects were monitored to ensure that they were not substituting CHSP services for others previously received. Fears that formal services would reduce the level of informal (typically familial) support proved unfounded.

Participants were expected to pay some part of the costs of meals and services, but it was left to each project to determine the copayment schemes. The early evaluation noted wide fluctuations in the source of service funding over time and across sites: roughly 20 percent of services were funded by other government programs, 75 percent were funded by CHSP, and the remaining 5 percent were financed directly by tenant fees. Thus participants generally paid less than $25 per month for services received, again with low marginal costs and little incentive to conserve on services.

In 1987, HUD made a number of important program changes. It standardized the copayment mechanism to include a sliding fee scale incorporating a minimum fee of 10 percent of the participant's adjusted monthly income. Combined with a required contribution of 30 percent of the participant's adjusted income for rent, this change means that CHSP participants are paying a minimum of 40 percent of income for the package of housing and support services. HUD also reduced the mandatory meal requirement to seven per week in response to the high proportion (over 50 percent) of meal costs and to participant complaints that many neither wanted nor required so many congregate meals.

In theory, this second change will reduce overservicing, promote independence, and free resources for other needed services. But experience suggests that a minimum of one meal a day should be a core service, and cutbacks should not be carried too far. Service coordinators and case managers report that mealtime is a vital opportunity to observe the health and functioning of frail residents daily. Moreover, because congregate dining operations require some minimum regular client base to be viable and cost-effective, some mandatory, or at least reliable, minimum participation is probably necessary. At most projects, meals may also be purchased by non-CHSP residents at cost; these economies of scale can be important in helping reduce the per-meal cost to the program.

As with meals, minimum viable participation limits apply to the larger program itself, especially to services requiring on-site staff. HUD has set 20 participants as the lower limit for justifying a full-time coordinator. The program may need cooperation from the housing manager to maintain minimum size as vacancies occur, possibly involving separate waiting lists for CHSP and non-CHSP vacancies within a building.

Currently, 60 CHSP projects serve some 1,920 persons in 33 states. The $5.4 million appropriation provided for fiscal year 1989 will extend operations of all projects until at least April 1990.

APPLICABLE FEDERAL FUNDING STREAMS

States may use three federal funding streams to help fund supportive service programs for low-income elderly in assisted housing. These resources impose varying levels of federal control. The discussion here helps set the context for the possible models of federal-state outlined cooperation in chapter 6.

One of the stated purposes of Social Services Block Grants (SSBG), administered by the Department of Health and Human Services (HHS) as the successor to Title XX, is "preventing or reducing inappropriate institutional care by providing for community-based care, home-based care, or other less intensive care" (Gaberlavage 1987, 1). The funding level for 1987 and future years is set at $2.7 billion, allocated to the states on the basis of population with no matching requirement. Forty-seven states currently use some part of their SSBG funds on services to the elderly. Among these states, the proportion of SSBG funds spent on elderly services ranged from 1 to 50 percent (Gaberlavage 1987), with a national average of 18 percent ($486 million nationwide). Funds are usually administered by a state department of social or human services with minimal federal control and reporting requirements. States are largely free to design their own mix of services and set their own standards and eligibility requirements.

Typical services currently funded include homemaker, companionship, and home maintenance, although most services offered under CHSP can also be funded by SSBG. SSBG monies may not be used for medical care, construction, major capital improvements, or room and board. Targeting of services to low-income and/or at-risk clients is usual but is no longer specifically required. Most states restrict some services by income and provide others (especially information and referral) without regard to income (Rabin and Stockton 1987). Twenty-six states impose a cost-sharing fee schedule for recipients.

States have been tightening income restrictions and increasing cost sharing to help offset budgetary constraints, but many report much qualified need going unmet and long waiting lists for services. Small declines in spending mask larger declines in the number of elderly served. Some states, of course, have shown a readiness to supplement SSBG funds with their own (as required under the old Title XX arrangement) to maintain former service levels. Nonetheless, the typical experience is that, facing constraints, states maintain mandated protective services at the expense of preventive and independence-fostering services such as those for the elderly (Coalition on Human Needs 1986). With the former already taking up more than 80 percent of SSBG funds nationwide and with funding capped at 1987 levels, there is reason to believe that money available for supportive services to the elderly under the SSBG program may gradually diminish. Cognizant of these constraints, and contingent on continued federal SSBG appropriations, states may still commit future SSBG funds to a service project. Under current law, HHS cannot earmark SSBG funds for congregate services, however, and states vary considerably in their use of these funds for such purposes.

The Older Americans Act (OAA) is another applicable federal resource "intended to assist older persons attain maximum independence in a home environment, to remove individual and social barriers to economic and personal independence, and to provide services and care for the vulnerable elderly" (U.S. Senate, Special Committee on Aging 1986, 338). Title III of the OAA provides grants for state and community programs on aging. Allocated to states based on their share of the nation's over-60 population, Title III funds are mostly passed on to AAAs, with a small allocation for state administration.

Title III funds are allocated separately for supportive services and senior centers (III B), congregate and home-delivered meals (III C), nonmedical in-home services for the frail elderly (III D), and assistance for special needs (III E). (See table 4.1.) The new categories, III D and III E, were authorized in 1987 and thus far only IIID has received funding. States are permitted to transfer up to 30 percent of funds among the categories. In FY 1986, for example, $47 million was transferred from the congregate nutrition appropriation to other Title III services (U.S. Senate, Special Committee on Aging 1987).

Under Title V, community service employment for older people also receives substantial funding. In 1985, roughly 40 percent of these jobs were in services to other elderly. Although three-quarters of Title V funds go to various national organizations instead of to states or AAAs, at least one state reported hiring elderly tenants up to 20 hours per week for supportive services to frailer residents in the same building. Creative states may thus be able to access Title V funds to help defray some of the costs of a supportive service program.

TABLE 4.1   DISTRIBUTION OF OLDER AMERICANS ACT
TITLE III BUDGET AUTHORITY, FY 1989

	Appropriations ($ millions)	Percentage of Title III Total
Supportive services and senior centers	$277	32.2
Nutrition services		
Congregate	357	41.6
Home delivered	79	9.2
Department of Agriculture commodities	141	16.4
In-home frail elderly services	5	.6
Total	$859	100.0%

Source: Unpublished figures supplied by R. Turman, Office of Management and Budget.

Although "[t]he law requires that preference be given to serving older persons with the greatest social or economic needs with particular attention to low income minority older persons, . . . [m]eans tests as a criterion for participation are prohibited" (U.S. Senate, Special Committee on Aging 1987, 339). Many congregate services programs in assisted housing in fact use Title III assistance, especially for meal service. The OAA, however, prohibits the imposition of fees or copayments for Title III services. Congress has consistently rejected administration proposals for cost-sharing, fee-for-service, or means-testing arrangements for Title III programs (U.S. Senate, Special Committee on Aging 1987).

A further problem in using OAA funds to encourage additional programs or congregate projects is that Title III was never intended to be a major continuing source of funding for social services. Instead, funds are intended to serve as seed money for developing an improved service infrastructure, and service providers may not receive Title III funds for more than three years without special permission from administrators (Sherwood 1985).

Medicaid provides three options for funding home and community-based services to the elderly. Under each, the Health Care Financing Administration (HCFA) is required to match state funding at a rate based on the state's per capita income. The state share of Medicaid costs ranges from 17 to 50 percent. Additionally, states may require local jurisdictions to pay up to 60 percent of the nonfederal share.

This first option is the Medicaid state plan, under which states may elect to provide in-home medical services to needy clients as additional regular benefits. Personal care services--including meal preparation, shopping, and dressing--qualify as long as they are "medically oriented," that is, prescribed by a physician to address a medical need, supplied by a qualified provider, and supervised by a registered nurse. Significantly, if states elect to provide these services, they must do so to all eligible Medicaid recipients.

As of 1984, 20 states covered some in-home personal care services under their state Medicaid programs (Burwell 1986). By far the largest of these was New York, which now spends nearly $1 billion annually on personal care services for some 60,000 clients, some of whom are elderly. New York accounts for more than three-quarters of such Medicaid spending and clientele nationwide. Growth in the program has been uncontrolled in recent years, and a shortage of home health providers has left the state unable to keep up with the demand.

The second option is known as the Section 2176 Home and Community-Based Services Medicaid waiver.[3] The 2176 waivers are a significant shift away from exclusively medical services, permitting states to offer a broader range of services without the stringent and expensive medical justification and monitoring requirements of the state plan option. Moreover, states also have considerable latitude to determine who receives services, with many of the usual requirements waived. States can set income levels, frailty definitions (although recipients are supposed to meet the level of care criteria for nursing home admission) and referral sources, and they can limit service to certain areas of the state (Burwell 1986).

The key prerequisite for 2176 waiver approval, however, is that the state must demonstrate to HCFA that spending on waiver services will be offset by at least commensurate savings to Medicaid on nursing home expenditures. HCFA demands in this regard have become increasingly exacting since the waiver program was enacted in 1981. As a consequence, state waiver programs have not grown as once expected, and many have become smaller. Because demonstrable savings from waivered home and community-based service programs and projected Medicaid spending increases due to nursing home care have both diminished in HCFA's eyes, the amount a state can spend on waivered services has also diminished. Further, "[s]tates are constrained from serving more individuals under the 2176 waiver than they would have done in its absence. . . . Waivers do not therefore create a statewide entitlement to any program and, in many cases, cover only a small number of eligible persons in selected areas" (Rabin and Stockton 1987, 223).

As of 1987, 46 states had at least one 2176 waiver program (Rabin and Stockton 1987). Only about three-quarters of them provided services to the elderly, with a total of some 60,000 elderly and disabled persons served nationwide (HHS, HCFA 1987). Total 1985 spending for the 2176 waiver programs was $312 million (in 1987 dollars), but modest growth was expected.

The third Medicaid option was created when Section 4102 of the Omnibus Budget Reconciliation Act of 1987 amended Title XIX of the Social Security Act to create a new Medicaid waiver authority (Section 1915(d)) specific to the elderly. States may now choose this option instead of the 2176 waiver. While allowing for substantially the same services as the existing waiver, the new program relaxes prior requirements to demonstrate the cost-effectiveness of a program. Instead, it aggregates federal Medicaid expenditures for nursing facility, home, and community-based services in a state for a base year and then increases the permissible total in subsequent years by factoring in increases in the cost of relevant goods and services, the over-75 population, and the intensity of services required (U.S. Senate, Special Committee on Aging 1987). The states divide this total between institutional and noninstitutional care as they see fit.

The main catch is that for a state choosing the new option, federal Medicaid matching is no longer openended. States gain freedom to design their own long-term care continuum and to distribute Medicaid clients within it; in return, they accept a reasonably indexed ceiling on federal matching for long-term care. Section 4102 essentially carves from Medicaid a long term care block grant for participating states. Medicaid's institutional bias can thus be gradually reduced at a state's discretion, enabling substantially increased home- and community-based service spending. States can expect to gain both flexibility and stability from the new waiver authority because waiver applications will no longer be subject to refusal by HCFA.

Only Oregon has opted for the 4102 waiver. It was Oregon in fact that lobbied Congress to create the waiver, which is also known as the Oregon waiver. So far, other states have a wait-and-see attitude. Participation necessitates considerable faith on the part of a state in its system of long-term care and its ability to take advantage of the option to serve its long-term-care population better and more cost-effectively.

For reference, total Medicaid spending on home health care under the first two Medicaid options in 1986 was about $1.4 billion (in 1987 dollars), compared to $17.3 billion in 1987 Medicaid expenditures on nursing home care, a potentially large pot of money to which home and congregate service programs may gain access as they are demonstrated to be effective.

SUMMARY

HUD's Congregate Housing Services Program and, less so, the joint FmHA/AoA congregate demonstration provide experience that the federal government could draw on in designing or expanding the direct provision of supportive services to the frail elderly in assisted housing. Many of the lessons learned in these programs are incorporated in the recommendations in chapter 7.

Social Services Block Grants, Title III funds, and Medicaid are all possible federal funding sources that the states could use to pay for supportive services (see chapter 3) or that the federal government could use to entice more states to offer supportive services (see chapter 6). Each source has current legislative constraints that limit its applicability, however. SSBG funds cannot be earmarked by the federal government for certain uses that it wants to promote. Second, in the competition for SSBG funds, supportive services for the elderly tend to receive second priority, behind more urgent and mandated protective services for children and others.

Title III funds have traditionally focused on nutrition services. Although the present structure of the Older Americans Act could accommodate a range of other supportive services, funding would have to be substantially reallocated or the states given broader discretion. Second, Title III is currently set up to provide seed money for service programs for up to three years. This mission would have to be modified for Title III to be used to provide major ongoing assistance to specific supportive service programs.

Medicaid seems to be evolving to accommodate the use of home and community-based service options. Still, Medicaid is primarily assistance for medical needs. It may be more appropriately viewed as the next level of care on the continuum for those who become too frail to be served just by supportive service programs. If this additional medical care can also be provided in home instead of or besides the more limited congregate services, so much the better. At present, administrators of supportive service programs are reluctant to tap into Medicaid sources because of the stringent medical licensing and supervision standards. If and when supportive service programs are shown to help delay and/or prevent institutionalization in a cost-effective manner, both state and federal governments will increasingly adapt their Medicaid programs to noninstitutional settings.

Chapter 5 reviews possible new approaches to support services in assisted housing, and chapter 6 addresses how best to access and use existing federal funding sources to generate federal-state cooperation in providing support services to the frail elderly. Advisable modifications to these funding sources are discussed in chapter 7.

Notes, chapter 4

1.   This and the other federal programs summarized in this chapter are described at greater length in appendix E. The description of the FmHA/AoA demonstration is based on Cronin, Drury, Gragg, et al. (1983).

2.   The three are "OARS," the "PISCES," and the Hebrew Rehabilitation Center for the Aged's "Community Support Potential" index. For more on indices, see, for example, Kane and Kane (1981); McDowell and Newell (1987); and Duke University Center (1978).

3.   Section 2176 of the Omnibus Budget Reconciliation Act of 1981 amended Title XIX (Section 1915(c)) of the Social Security Act. Thus this waiver is also known as a Medicaid Section 1915(c) waiver.

POSSIBLE NEW APPROACHES

Previous chapters describe state and federally funded housing programs that also provide support services. This chapter introduces three new models of service delivery programs, which could either operate in parallel with or substitute for the congregate housing models already discussed. Under all three, providers would receive roughly fixed payments for assisting the frail elderly with needed support services. And under one, vendors would compete with each other for clients. Proponents of the approaches expect these features to control costs and improve service quality levels compared with the traditional congregate models.

The first model is the Housing and Support Services Certificate Program (HSSCP), which provides a certificate for frail elders judged to need support services who are already participating in a federal housing assistance program. The local administering agency would arrange for services using the funds commanded by the certificate. Beneficiaries would contribute at least 10 percent of their incomes to defray service costs.

The second program, now in the demonstration phase, deviates somewhat from more housing-oriented models. Social/health maintenance organizations (S/HMOs) provide prepaid health coverage along with limited long-term-care services. Although this program does not have a specific housing orientation, it could be applied in any of the assisted housing environments. It has developed procedures for determining eligibility criteria, targeting and marketing techniques, methods for tailoring services, and methods for case management. It provides services on a capitated basis; essentially, the customer buys insurance coverage for various services. A capitation fee is a fixed fee paid to a program from which a set array of services is available, as opposed to paying separately for each service used.

As suggested, an advantage to this model is that it does not depend on a central housing location for service provision; it, like the HSSCP, could be used in a multitude of housing situations: elderly-only projects, aged-mixed (family) projects, and scattered facilities, as under the Section 8 Existing and the voucher programs. For those in assisted housing, some of the fees associated with being "insured" would be paid through subsidies from the housing or health agency to the S/HMO; the balance would come from participant copayments. All elderly occupants of assisted housing in a locality would be enrolled, regardless of whether they needed services at the time of enrollment.

The third model is the Congregate Housing Certificate Program (CHCP). It would provide those eligible in terms of income and frailty a single voucher good for both housing and support services in exchange for a stipulated share of income. The vouchers could be used at approved privately operated congregate facilities, which would compete for clients. These projects would be expected to house market-rate as well as assisted households.

HOUSING AND SUPPORT SERVICES CERTIFICATE PROGRAM

The HSSCP simply provides a voucher for receipt of support services by residents of assisted housing assessed to have a level of impairment sufficient to need the services. Support services are provided to participants in their own units. The program can be viewed as applicable to frail elders participating in all federally assisted housing programs. Clearly, the HSSCP could easily be used to help those already receiving housing assistance because the HSSCP certificate is an "add on" to the existing housing assistance.

Several entities could be the local administering agency (LAA). Candidates include the local public housing authority (PHA) and nonprofit organizations experienced in housing and service provision for the elderly, including sponsors in the Section 202 program.

Under the HSSCP, the participant, after being screened for eligibility by the local agency, would receive a certificate good for support services. The LAA would use it to provide the necessary services. The LAA, rather than the person herself, arranges for services because of the difficulty some elderly persons have in making the arrangements and because of the "market power" the LAA would have in dealing with vendors.

Thus the responsibilities of the LAA would include case management and arranging for delivery of services. The LAA would work closely with state and local social service agencies in carrying out these responsibilities and could subcontract these duties to a vendor, including one of these agencies. The LAA could even contract with several vendors which could compete to serve certificate holders. This may particularly be an option where the public housing authority is the LAA, since the authority may have less experience in the delivery of support services.

However arranged, service provision would be subject to the budget constraints of the certificates. Whether the LAA discharged the service delivery and case management tasks directly or subcontracted, it is likely that the agency would need to augment or train its staff for these new responsibilities; creation of such a training program at the national level would have to be fully considered by the Department of Housing and Urban Development (HUD).

Setting the certificate value is obviously a critical design feature. It appears that this responsibility could be taken by HUD with advice from the Department of Health and Human Services (HHS).[1] In the broadest terms, HUD would set up a procedure parallel to that now employed to set the Fair Market Rents in the Section 8 Existing program. The value of the certificate would depend, among other factors, on local wage rates and the service packages provided to those receiving assistance.

In general, the service package should contain case management, housekeeping and periodic chore services, personal care, laundry assistance, transportation services, meal assistance, and, under some circumstances, congregate e of the services would be mandatory, with the eption of congregate meals that might be required in pi-ᵤⱼ with a concentration of residents needing meal services. In short, establishing the value of the certificate would require determining both reasonable quantities of services to meet the needs of persons with an "average" degree of frailty and the price of those services in local markets. As is discussed in chapter 6, the current range among states of the costs of providing one month of support services is large, in part because of differences in the package and quantity of services provided. Thus it is clear that setting the service levels with any degree of precision--an element essential for any national program requiring such a capitated benefit level--is a significant task.

Participants would contribute a minimum of 10 percent of their incomes for services. Higher income shares would be required of those receiving higher levels of services, although a maximum, perhaps of 20 percent, would be imposed. At the same time, participants would be guaranteed a reasonable amount of income remaining after their monthly contributions for essential expenditures.

The HSSCP has two attractive features in the current context. One is its widespread applicability to the population of frail elders already in assisted housing. The second is the fact that because it is a capitated system (i.e., the LAA receives a fixed amount for each person participating), there are strong incentives for the efficient delivery of services.

SOCIAL/HEALTH MAINTENANCE ORGANIZATIONS

The Health Care Financing Administration (HCFA) social/health maintenance organization (S/HMO) demonstration is designed to test both the expansion of prepaid coverage of community and nursing home care in a controlled manner and the linkage of these expanded services with a complete acute care system. To accomplish this goal, the four demonstration sites (Brooklyn, New York; Portland, Oregon; Long Beach, California; and Minneapolis, Minnesota) were to follow four guidelines: (1) a single organizational structure was to provide a complete range of acute and chronic care services, (2) a coordinated case management system was to be used to ensure access to appropriate services, (3) enrollment in S/HMOs was to include a mix of frail and able-bodied elderly, and (4) the organizations were to be financed on a prepaid capitated basis through a combination of monthly premiums from Medicare, Medicaid, and enrollees.[2]

The four sites began operating in March 1985. As of the spring of 1987, they had a total enrollment of more than 11,000 Medicare beneficiaries. All sites offer all Medicare-covered services plus other expanded services. Expanded care includes personal care, homemaker service, day care, respite care, transportation, and institutional care.

The HCFA supported an evaluation of the early experience of the S/HMOs. Although the final report has not been released, the balance of this section draws on related papers prepared by those doing the evaluation and by other analysts.

Two models were developed for the S/HMO demonstration project. The sites in Portland (Kaiser Permanente) and Minneapolis (Seniors Plus) are sponsored by established HMOs, thus functioning as new benefit programs for existing health maintenance organizations (HMOs). The sites in Brooklyn (Elderplan) and Long Beach (SCAN Health Plan) were developed as new HMOs by long-term-care organizations.

Similar to a health maintenance organization, the S/HMO uses capitation fees (a set fee paid in advance) and provides health and long-term-care services. (HMOs provide only health services.) Although the HMOs have the incentive of providing adequate low-cost outpatient care to prevent higher-cost hospitalization, the S/HMOs have the incentive of providing a combination of lower-cost outpatient care as well as long-term-care services to prevent high-cost hospitalization and institutionalization. Limitations are set on the amount of chronic care services available to a member, and a copayment has been required at all sites for all home care.

The monthly member premiums for the programs range from $29.50 to $49.00: Seniors Plus, $29.50; Elderplan, $29.89; SCAN, $40.00; and Kaiser, $49.00. For reference, note that the minimum 10 percent of income now charged for services in the Congregate Housing Services Program would be about $60 per month for the average elderly occupant of assisted housing.

Developers of the S/HMO project recognized that because the chronic care benefits of the program were not offered within the competing Medicare supplement market, there was a good possibility that the program might be especially attractive to the already disabled population. But because financing for chronic care benefits in S/HMOs comes from private premiums and savings on hospital services, for the S/HMOs to be financially viable, they need a membership that is no more impaired than a cross-section of the aged population.

With the intent of keeping the S/HMO population from becoming overrepresented by severely disabled persons, HCFA agreed to allow the demonstration sites to queue their applicants according to their self-reported disability status. Quotas were established using national and regional data on the prevalence of severe and moderate disability. Disability was based on answers to questions on the applications. Sites were allowed to close enrollment to the severely impaired when proportions exceeded 4-5 percent of new members. For the moderately disabled, enrollment closed when proportions exceeded 10-17 percent. Those who were closed out were placed on waiting lists. Although none of the sites ended up with queues for the moderately impaired group, all sites except for Kaiser queued for the severely disabled.

It is possible that the elderly population in assisted housing in a particular area would be more frail than the population at large. For this or other reasons (such as the mix of services provided), the S/HMO and PHA might agree that the elderly in assisted housing are a separate risk group with its own fee structure.

Although the S/HMOs all followed the same basic screening and assessment procedures, no standard eligibility criteria were set. And although each site developed its own eligibility criteria for receipt of expanded care benefits, all used nursing home certifiable (NHC) status in some way. NHC criteria were developed to determine eligibility for state Medicaid coverage in nursing homes. Nursing home certifiability, therefore, does not suggest that an individual should be in a nursing home. Each state used different criteria to determine NHC status. In California, clinical judgment determines NHC status; in New York and Oregon, activity of daily living (ADL) levels and mental capacity are used. An individual with a deficiency in only one ADL is considered nursing home certifiable in some states.

The S/HMO sites used three strategies to determine eligibility for expanded care services: strictly limiting expanded care benefits to NHC-eligible members (Kaiser and Elderplan), providing expanded care to those who are NHC eligible as well as to the moderately disabled (SCAN), and using the NHC eligibility but allowing exceptions based on the judgment of case managers and the S/HMO director (Seniors Plus).

The initial enrollment goal per site was 4,000 clients in the first 12-18 months. This high goal was set to provide an adequate sample size of all groups in the case mix and an enrollment level at which sites could break even on costs. As of December 1986 (21 months), enrollment at the four sites was: Elderplan, 2,571; Kaiser, 4,305; SCAN, 2,062; and Seniors Plus, 1,688 (Greenberg et al., 1988). Only Kaiser reached the enrollment goal.

Several studies present possible explanations for the low enrollment in S/HMOs (Greenberg et al. 1988; Harrington, Newcomer, and Friedlob 1988a; and Rivlin and Wiener 1988). First, many people mistakenly believe that they are sufficiently covered by insurance and therefore S/HMO enrollment is not worth the extra money. Second, those who waited until they were disabled to enroll were closed out of the program because of the high enrollment of disabled people. Third, sponsorship by long-term-care organizations negatively affects perceptions of the program by the unimpaired, who identify S/HMOs with chronic illness and dependency. Fifth, the elderly are reluctant to change physicians and are not happy with where some of the primary and acute care facilities are located. Finally, other more limited programs' premiums are lower and are marketed more competitively.

Marketing S/HMOs may be a problem in assisted housing for many of the same reasons. If the S/HMO option were adopted in an area and a copayment by participants were included, then the plan would have to be marketed to elders living in assisted housing. As in the demonstration programs, it would be essential to enroll a good cross-section of the population. A key part of the marketing would be to make clear that no other assistance with support services would be available through the housing provider.

The role of the case managers in the S/HMO demonstration sites is to coordinate the comprehensive institutional and community-based long-term-care services that make up the chronic care benefit package. Thus they are in contact with acute care providers, informal caregivers, and non-S/HMO service providers involving legal help, social security, housing, provision of meals, and other social programs.

The organizational structure of the S/HMO affected the job of case managers. The two sites that were initially HMO affiliated left the responsibility and control over acute care with the HMO professionals. The sites developing their own HMOs assigned part of the utilization review and discharge planning responsibilities to the case mangers of the S/HMOs.

A large part of the case managers' responsibility, as discussed by Rivlin and Wiener (1988), is to control chronic care costs. They do so by encouraging substitution of in-home care for nursing home care, encouraging substitution of less expensive unskilled home help for relatively expensive skilled medical home care services, helping to avoid extended hospital stays for long-term-care patients who no longer have acute care needs, and ensuring that the use of nursing home and home care services is not extensive and that the costs of these services are competitive.

Revenues for all S/HMO sites come from a variety of sources. Although amounts varied by site, the sources were relatively consistent: premiums, copayments, Medicare-adjusted average per capita costs (AAPCC), Medicaid capitation, interest, and miscellaneous sources. In general, the largest share of total revenue came from the Medicare AAPCC payments (45-83 percent) and the next largest from premiums (11-19 percent).

Harrington, Newcomer, and Friedlob (1988b) examined the financial success of the S/HMOs during the first 24 months. Success was defined as providing S/HMO services while controlling use and expenditures to ensure the financial viability of the program. All sites except Kaiser overestimated their total revenues because Medicare and Medicaid enrollments were lower than expected. The extensive marketing needs were not anticipated, and these costs rose as sites attempted to reach their enrollment goals.

The high service costs for the two S/HMOs that developed their own HMOs were related to their high acute and ambulatory use. The two S/HMOs that were affiliated with existing HMOs were better able to control costs, using their experience in developing appropriate budgets. (See table 5.1.)

TABLE 5.1   FINANCIAL PROFILE OF S/HMO SITES

	Total Revenue	Total Expenditures	Net Gain or Loss
Elderplan			
1985	$ 1,633,024	$ 3,631,846	$-1,998,822
1986	5,726,551	9,120,503	-3,393,952
Kaiser			
1985	5,123,953	5,367,315	-243,430
1986	13,072,459	13,683,211	-610,752
SCAN			
1985	2,242,159	3,693,592	-1,451,433
1986	6,972,727	8,197,206	-1,224,479
Seniors Plus			
1985	679,751	1,203,272	-523,701
1986	3,534,260	4,508,478	-974,218

Source: Harrington, Newcomer, and Friedlob (1988b).

The losses were not unexpected, although they were larger than had been anticipated. According to Greenberg et al. (1988), the losses were due primarily to high marketing and sales budgets and administration that had not reached economies of scale, as opposed to an inappropriate scope of benefits or management inability. As the models are refined and developed, these losses may diminish. For new sites to be developed without incurring such large losses, however, a more detailed look at the specific costs to the program as they relate to the organizational models is necessary. Greenberg et al. (1988) and Harrington et al. (1988b) suggest that the more financially viable model may be the one in which long-term-care services are added to an existing HMO. It is important to keep in mind that the initial S/HMO losses were not too different from the experiences of the earliest HMOs.

A point made in one evaluation paper (Harrington et al. 1988b) is that at the two sites not initiated in an established HMO, planning and arranging for the delivery of acute and ambulatory services were more difficult than where an HMO was in place. Although some of these problems would be expected in any kind of new venture, this experience also demonstrates the point that health and long-term-care organizations may not find it so easy to gear up to provide a mixture of these services.

It would be feasible for residents of assisted housing to use the S/HMO programs. Using S/HMOs in all types of assisted housing is attractive. In addition, although Medicaid clients are eligible for S/HMO services, their enrollment is low. A special targeting effort to include a large group of elderly residents of assisted housing might provide the opportunity for evaluating the costs and benefits of using a S/HMO or S/HMO-like model with a publicly assisted population group.

One last note is the fact that the S/HMO and HSSCP models can come close to each other. Indeed, the PHAs could contract with S/HMOs to handle the entire frail elderly population in assisted housing population if HSSCP revenues could cover the government's share of the S/HMO fees.

THE CONGREGATE HOUSING CERTIFICATE PROGRAM

The CHCP, as described in Newman and Struyk (1987), is one of the conceptual models for providing both housing and supportive services to the frail elderly. An eligible household would receive a certificate entitling it to occupy an independent unit in a private congregate housing project that provides necessary support services on site. These services include a limited number of congregate meals, personal care services, homemaker services, laundry assistance, specialized transportation, and housekeeping services. The value of the certificate--based essentially on the Section 8 Fair Market Rent plus the cost of support services--would be set on a market-by-market basis. There might be two certificate levels corresponding to needs for services.[3] However, this strength is also a weakness because moving in some cases is a disruptive, disorienting experience for the elderly.

The housing would be a multiunit project with units fully equipped and specially designed to accommodate the elderly. Housing projects and support services would be privately developed, financed, owned, and operated, and they would be encouraged to serve voucher holders as well as households paying the market rate.

No predetermined mix of CHCP clients and paying tenants has been established. To be eligible for vouchers, households would have to meet income criteria for housing assistance, be 62 years of age or older, and be judged at high risk of being institutionalized according to a specific risk assessment tool. Vouchers would be redeemable only in approved projects, as opposed to use in a household's current home, and the program would endeavor to ensure that various options were open to certificate holders. At the time of application, households could be either homeowners or tenants. The mandatory condition is that regardless of their ownership status, they must be willing to move into the housing project. This condition is likely to result in an automatic screening out of those at lower risk of institutionalization and to attract those with a serious need for available services.

Potential recipients of CHCP vouchers would be certified by the local PHA, possibly working with state or local health agencies. Housing assistance income guidelines and the risk assessment tool used for the CHSP would be applied to determine eligibility. Given a list of approved congregate housing projects, the recipient household would then be responsible for deciding which among the different congregate facilities to move into. Once a client is admitted to a particular site, all further assessment would be done by the housing vendor. It is assumed that both a case manager and medical personnel would work together to tailor available services to individual needs. Recipients could move to another congregate facility whenever they wished, subject to the conditions of any lease they signed.

The costs of providing housing and support services are estimated at approximately $954 per month (in 1987 dollars), assuming that the housing facilities were built in 1985 (Heumann 1987). Assuming that a recipient contribution to these costs is about 50 percent of household income and occupant income is the same as that of the average elderly recipient of housing subsidies, the monthly subsidy would be $624 (Newman and Struyk 1987). Although a participant contribution of 50-60 percent of household income is presumed as a viable rate, this rate would prevail for a particular recipient only if such a level permitted reasonable expenditures on necessities.

In contrast to the other options, the CHCP organizations, private organizations operating on fixed budgets, will have to compete with other providers for clients; in many ways their reactions would be like those of S/HMOs. The restriction of fixed budgets gives both programs strong incentives to tailor their services to the needs of the clients at the lowest cost to the provider rather than to offer more services to clients.

The key features of the CHCP are the enhanced opportunity for clients to live in housing with services plus the rationalized administrative process and cost savings from joining housing and supportive services. There has been some recent movement toward using rent supplements (Section 8 Existing housing assistance certificates and housing vouchers) in more supportive living arrangements. Congress authorized two initiatives in 1983 that HUD is now implementing: the use of rent supplements in single room occupancy (SRO) arrangements and the use of rent supplements in shared living arrangements (Newman and Struyk 1987). The concept papers outlining the legislative plans of Senators Cranston and D'Amato circulated in the summer of 1988 discuss a voucher program for the handicapped with HUD providing housing certificates and the states providing services. Such a program falls short of the model outlined in CHCP because it fails to avoid the complicated procedures for obtaining and coordinating shelter and supportive services from different public agencies.

The CHCP may be of limited use for the current population of frail elders in assisted housing because they would have to move into a CHCP project to participate. Although some such movement is to be anticipated, it could be quite limited, depending on how badly services are needed and the extent to which they are otherwise available.

This discussion raises the more general potential problem of requiring relocation for participation in a project. Are the elderly willing to move? There is evidence that the residential mobility of the elderly increases at very high ages, often because increased frailty increases the difficulties of continued independent living in larger units (Meyer and Speare 1985). The design of the CHCP banks on this notion. However, the willingness of the elderly to move is sensitive to the location of projects (i.e., the nearer a project is to the neighborhood where the participant previously lived, the more attractive it is). Hence, if the CHCP model were tried, it would be essential to sign up many projects--at least 8-10 within a metropolitan area--to participate.

SUMMARY

As described above, the CHCP and S/HMO programs operate through private organizations, providing the elderly with options for health and/or long-term services while they live independently. Although CHCP provides only services for the frail elderly living in a specific congregate housing facility, the Housing and Support Services Certificate Program and S/HMO programs could enroll elderly living in any type of assisted housing. The S/HMO does not provide housing; however, it is the only option providing limited long-term institutional care. All programs provide for varying levels of in-home personal care.

All three programs could embody strong incentives, through capitated payments, to develop a case management system that will tailor the service package to meet clients' needs cost-effectively. None of the programs is designed to offer all services to all clients. Because CHSP and S/HMOs would be operated by private entities, the incentives for efficiency may be even greater.

Only in HSSCP might a government agency be involved directly in the operational aspects of service delivery. In CHCP and S/HMOs, government action would be limited to a financial subsidy for client services and general program oversight. For the S/HMOs, involvement would not include the need to determine the degree of frailty of the assisted housing elderly inasmuch as all enrollees are eligible. The responsibility for expanded care services would belong to the S/HMO or CHCP facility. The applicability of these models is discussed in chapter 7.

In closing, it is worth emphasizing that the three models outlined above have several features which could be combined in other ways to form a large array of somewhat differentiated programs. The more prominent tradeoffs or options include: assigning responsibility for obtaining services to the individual (participant) or a local administering agency; providing services in congregate facilities or a broader range of housing; integrating housing and support service payments or maintaining them separately; and using a tightly targeted system or one in which all elderly are eligible, like the S/HMO. The models presented above should be viewed as promising starting points and not finished products.

Notes, chapter 5

1.   Having HUD discharge this function and the general oversight role seems wise for several reasons. First, the HUD area offices have financial information on housing operations. With the data on supportive services, it would have a quite complete picture of the finances at each project--something essential for real oversight. Second, having HUD take the lead on setting costs and other functions minimizes the fragmentation in responsibility across agencies. Having said this, we acknowledge that parts of HHS could also discharge some of these functions.

2.   Life Care at Home (LCAH) is another capitated system of this type now being developed. It is less appropriate for the assisted housing population than S/HMOs because of its greater emphasis on funding institutional care. LCAH is described in appendix E.

3.   This feature would reduce the incentive for providers to accept relatively well patients for whom it would be cheaper to provide services.

MODELS OF FEDERAL-STATE COOPERATION

From the previous chapters, it is clear that initiatives at both federal and state levels contribute importantly to the fund of knowledge about the design of alternative systems for the provision of supportive services. Both levels of government stand to reap significant financial benefits if provision of supportive services proves a cost-effective part of the long-term-care system. This chapter addresses federal-state cooperation in funding supportive services provision.

In terms of sources of funds from "housing agencies," some states have recently established housing trust funds based on earmarked tax sources that might be tapped (Nenno and Colyer 1988). Another possible source is the substantial reserves that some state housing finance agencies have been able to assemble, but such states are in the minority. Indeed, most states have yet to experiment with supportive service programs directly linked to assisted housing. As detailed below, funds from social service programs hold more promise.

This situation has two fundamental implications for identifying which models of federal-state cooperation may be viable over at least the next few years. First, it will be necessary for the federal government to provide significant incentives to increase the number of participating states and to reinforce the commitment of states that have shown early interest. Second, reliable sources of state funds must be found that are common to all states. In the absence of knowledge about what those funding sources might be on a state-by-state basis, the focus here is on federal funds controlled in whole or in part by the states.[1] They include funds from Social Services Block Grants (SSBG), Title III of the Older Americans Act, and Medicaid, both the main program and the waivered options.

In the balance of this chapter, three federal-state funding models are explored:

1. the federal government's contributing certain forms
of housing assistance and states contributing the
supportive services to the frail elderly occupying these
units,

2. federal-state funding of supportive services from
the savings in Medicaid expenditures that may accrue
from delayed institutionalization of the frail elderly,
and

3. federal-state funding of services for federal and
state assisted housing units occupied by frail elderly
persons independent of any linkage created through
Medicaid savings.

For the first and third models, a key consideration is the length
of time for which funds for the necessary supportive services
could be committed by both the federal and state governments.

The discussion of these models is independent of the
particular delivery system used. Note, however, that the
social/health maintenance organizations (S/HMOs) and the
certificate programs discussed in chapter 5 could be used, as
could the more conventional methods. The final section of the
chapter examines the cost of serving the frail elderly now in
assisted housing and compares it with the monies in SSBG and
Title III controlled by the states.

FEDERAL ASSISTED HOUSING AND STATE SUPPORTIVE SERVICES

The basic model here would be for the Department of Housing
and Urban Development (HUD) to fund additional units of
housing for elderly occupancy through its existing subsidy
programs and for the states to fund the necessary supportive
services for the units occupied by the frail elderly who require
them. Receipt of the additional units would be conditioned on
a state's willingness to commit to this funding responsibility.
This idea is similar to one set forth in the summer of 1988 in
the concept papers describing the features of new housing

legislation that may be introduced by Senators Cranston and D'Amato.

This model might be termed the "specialization model" because both the federal government and the states are executing roles traditional to each. The contributions of the two partners to total costs are difficult to estimate without more program details. The cost of a unit month of housing services varies sharply, depending on whether development of the unit is subsidized or whether the unit is in the existing stock and rented with assistance through a rent subsidy; subsidies for development are much higher than rent supplements for existing units. Although the cost of a month of supportive services is known, it is unclear in the case of a designated "frail elderly" project what share of the additional units would be occupied by recipients of supportive services. HUD guidelines for the Congregate Housing Services Program (CHSP) suggest one in four or five. An arrangement with HUD funding new units and states assisting only one occupant in five would provide attractive incentives for state participation. Clearly less attractive to states would be vouchers from HUD used mostly by frail households needing supportive services.

A major limitation of this specialization model is that it applies only to additional units. It simultaneously expands the number of assisted housing units with supportive services and the number of households in assisted housing needing those services. Hence, it does not address the need for supportive services of the frail elderly living in the existing inventory of assisted housing. Given the number of frail elderly at risk of institutionalization, this failure is a serious problem. It could be dealt with to some extent through the transfer of those needing services into the additional units, but this approach depends heavily on the services already available to these people. Hence, the model would have to be complemented by another--possibly the third model sketched below or through funding more projects under the CHSP--to take care of the existing population.

A key question is whether the states could pay for the needed support services from the federal funds at their disposal or leverage other resources for these services. Service costs, which can be estimated independent of the housing setting (new or existing), depend on the size of the population to be served. Because the number of additional units to be provided under this specialization model and the share of frail elderly occupying them are impossible to predict here, our discussion assumes the current number of elderly occupants of federally assisted housing in each state estimated to be at risk of being institutionalized. The states' cost of serving this population and the adequacy of SSBG and Title III funds for these purposes are examined in detail later in this chapter.

FEDERAL-STATE COOPERATION THROUGH POSSIBLE MEDICAID SAVINGS

If the provision of supportive services to the frail elderly were consistently effective in delaying the institutional placement of the elderly, then considerable savings could accrue to the federal and state governments.[2] Realization of such net savings are doubtful, however, for reasons given below. Many advocates of supportive housing argue that the demonstration of actual savings is not the point. Instead, any reduction in the cost of Medicaid-funded institutionalization (even if not a net savings in total long-term-care expenditures) associated with supportive housing should be recognized, as should its broader benefits for participants--higher morale and greater life satisfaction.

The conditions under which significant reductions in Medicaid costs might be realized are somewhat complex. Hence, this section begins by discussing these conditions. It then illustrates how much states might be willing to contribute to supportive housing under various assumptions about Medicaid cost reductions.

Two broad conditions are necessary for achieving significant cost reductions in Medicaid payments for nursing home care through supportive housing. First, the targeting of supportive services must be good (i.e., the elderly who would remain in the community without the benefit of these services must not receive them).

Viewed in this way, success in targeting is limited to the extent that supportive services merely substitute for other forms of care and assistance that frail individuals rely on in order to remain in the community and also to the extent that services are used by people who are not currently at risk, i.e., would not otherwise be in institutions. Some evidence on the size and nature of this substitution effect is found in a number of community care demonstrations, including most prominently the National Long-Term-Care Channeling Demonstration, known generally as channeling. Using a randomized experimental design and operating in 10 states and local sites, one purpose of the demonstration was to determine the extent to which formally provided, community-based long-term-care services such as case management, personal care, and homemaker services displaced informal caregiving by family and friends (Kemper 1988). Two community care service models were tested. Both included comprehensive case management. But one--the basic case management model--had access to some limited additional funds to fill gaps in the existing service system, whereas the other--the financial control model--gave case managers the authority to connect clients to needed services regardless of whether categorical eligibility requirements for the receipt of services were met. Overall, substitution effects on informal caregiving were found to be small. The basic model generated no such effects; the financial model was associated with substitution in some areas (e.g., help with household chores such as housework and laundry, help with meal preparation, delivery of prepared meals, and transportation) but not others (e.g., personal care and medical treatments).

The second condition necessary for cost reductions is that any savings realized by supportive housing must not be eaten up by the release of excess demand in the system. Some analysts contend that savings of this type are unlikely to materialize because the limited supply of nursing home beds in the past several years has built up an excess demand for these beds. In this case, delaying the institutionalization of some elderly would simply mean that others would occupy the nursing home beds. This argument does not appear valid, even currently, at least on a nationwide basis, because there are at least two important differences among states in current practices, indicating that real savings are possible at least in some states. First, although the supply of nursing home beds per elderly person declined in many states from 1981 to 1985, it expanded in 15 states, and by more than 25 percent in 4. So at least in 15 states, the excess demand argument is questionable. Second, in states where the bed shortage is a binding constraint, this constraint is producing other long-term-care costs: (a) delays in the release of patients from acute care facilities because nursing home beds cannot be found, (b) more extensive use of acute care facilities because more frail elderly are at home where fewer medical services are available, and (c) the use of 2176 Medicaid waivers to circumvent the nursing home bed limits by authorizing equivalent care (at approximately equal costs) in the community. The first two cost increases, which are large on a per-day basis, are borne by Medicare; the states are not required to contribute to these costs, but they are very real for the federal government and taxpayers. States do share directly in 2176 waiver costs.

The general point of the foregoing is that in some states it seems likely that the "long-term-care system" has found ways to provide substitutes for nursing home beds when supply is restricted. It is these costs as well as strictly nursing home expenditures that could be reduced through supportive housing. Moreover, over the longer term, many analysts, including Rivlin and Wiener (1988), simply do not believe that the supply of nursing home beds will be significantly restricted.

The required target efficiency for programs providing supportive services to achieve savings is illustrated by the figures in table 6.1 for the Congregate Housing Services Program and the Congregate Housing Certificate Program (CHCP) computed for 1985 and adjusted to 1987 dollar values. The table shows per-month subsidy figures for these programs given various tenant contribution rates (i.e., as a share of income). The contribution rates are set to provide a range of outcomes; note, for example, that the effective average total contribution rate under CHSP is probably about 35-38 percent, including 25-28 percent for housing alone.[2a]

TABLE 6.1   TARGETING REQUIREMENTS FOR SUPPORTIVE
HOUSING SUBSIDIES TO BE LESS THAN NURSING
HOME SUBSIDIES

Program and Tenant Contribution

	CHSP		CHCP
	t=.30[a]	t-.55[a]	t=.55[a]
Subsidies per month			
Nursing home	$940	$940	$940
Congregate facility[b]	649	485	622
Difference	292	455	318
Targeting rate for "break even"[c]			
Perfect nursing home targeting efficiency	1.45	1.94	1.51
80% nursing home targeting efficiency[d]	1.53	2.13	1.61

a.   Effective contribution rates as a share of income, allowing for adjustments to gross incomes.
b.   Includes subsidies for both housing and supportive services.
c.   Computed as the nursing home subsidy divided by the congregate facility subsidy. The figure is the maximum number of people in supportive housing for each one in supportive housing who is being kept out of an institution.
d.   Assumes that 20 percent of those in nursing homes need only and receive the levels of services in CHSP. The cost of correctly placed nursing home resident services are increased accordingly.

The monthly savings in government subsidies per person in a supportive housing facility compared to a nursing home range from $292 to $455 (in 1987 prices), depending on the costs and participant contribution rate selected. Compared to the $940 monthly subsidy cost for a nursing home, these figures suggest that if nursing homes took in only those needing this level of services, then supportive housing facilities could serve an extra 45-94 persons for every 100 who would otherwise be in a nursing home, and they would still be cost-effective. If we relax the assumption about targeting efficiency in nursing homes to 80 percent (i.e., 20 percent of the occupants need a lower level of care), then between 53 and 113 "extra" persons could be served in congregate facilities and the overall cost would still not be greater than that of nursing homes per person properly treated. These targeting requirements would be relaxed somewhat more if account were taken of the substitution of supportive services provided by CHSP or CHCP for some services already being provided.

These figures may suggest that the targeting requirements on congregate facilities are not stringent. To the contrary, the results of various demonstrations of community-based long-term care, including the channeling demonstrations, indicate that it is extremely difficult to target long-term-care services provided in the community to those who are truly at risk of being institutionalized (Weissert 1985). In these terms, the requirements just listed are demanding. Although the targeting rate of current congregate housing programs is not known, based on the eligibility criteria and assessment procedures, it is doubtful that the rates are more than half those shown in the table (i.e., three or more persons may be receiving services for each one whose entry into a nursing home is being delayed).

States share the cost of Medicaid with the federal government. Matching rates range from 18 to 50 percent, with the vast majority in the 30-50 percent range. Table 6.2 shows the maximum dollar amounts per month and the matching rates (the share of nursing home subsidies) that states could be willing to pay for each supportive housing service unit under different assumptions about the state Medicaid matching rate and the target efficiency of the supportive housing program. More specifically, it is the maximum payment per month that the state would be willing to make for each person living in supportive housing. So, for example, a state with a 30 percent matching rate would be willing to pay up to $171 per month to

TABLE 6.2   MAXIMUM STATE CONTRIBUTIONS TO A SUPPORTIVE HOUSING PROGRAM UNDER DIFFERENT STATE MEDICAID MATCHING RATES AND CONGREGATE TARGET EFFICIENCIES

	Medicaid Matching Rate		
	.25	.30	.50
Monthly dollar amounts[a]			
"Break even" targeting	$142	$171	$285
Targeting at 80% of "break even"	114	137	228
Targeting at 50% of "break even"	68	86	142
Matching rates[b]			
"Break even" matching	.25	.30	.50
Targeting at 80% of "break even"	.20	.24	.40
Targeting at 50% of "break even"	.12	.15	.25

a.   The "break even" or cost-neutral targeting rate is assumed to be 1.65 people receiving supportive services for each one whose nursing home entry is delayed, based on the figures in the lower panel of table 6.1. The dollar amounts in the first row of this table are computed as the product of (a) the maximum monthly total (state and federal) subsidy per person receiving supporting service, which is computed as the nursing home subsidy divided by the targeting rate (i.e., $940/1.65), and (b) the state's matching rate. Figures in the other rows are computed as the product of (a) and the state matching rate adjusted for poorer targeting; these factors are shown in the lower panel of this table.
b.   The figures in the first row are simply the state Medicaid matching rate. Figures in the lower rows are adjusted for targeting performance. For example, for states with a 25 percent matching rate, the figure in the second row for 80 percent "break even" targeting is .25 x .8 (= .20).

a supportive housing facility for each of 1.65 units for the nursing home bed kept empty if it believed that a housing unit would contain a person who would otherwise have been in a nursing home 60 percent of the time. In this case, the federal contribution would be $570 per month per person (given the 70:30 matching rate). The total funds available would then be $741 per month--sufficient to meet the total subsidy cost of supportive housing shown in table 6.1. Of course, at lower target efficiency, full subsidies of supportive housing cannot be covered.[3]

The proportion of frail elderly in assisted housing receiving supportive services whose receipt of those services is in fact instrumental in delaying their placement in an institution is obviously crucial. The data from the CHSP evaluation suggest that this proportion is low. But problems with the evaluation, as well as program changes (made since the evaluation) designed to increase its target efficiency, make these data an unreliable guide. Even so, a 30-40 percent rate still seems generous. The figures shown in chapter 2 on the relation between institutional placement and a person needing assistance with at least one activity of daily living (ADL) suggest that only one frail person in three is really being kept out of an institution. Obviously, strong evidence is not in yet, and more refined estimates are essential for actual decision-making. On the basis of the suggestive figures at hand, one would not be sanguine about net savings being large, or even positive.

In this context, it is useful to note that the same general logic applies for states (e.g., New York) that are choosing to supplement Supplemental Security Income (SSI) payments to pay for services necessary to delay institutionalization. States fund these supplements in large part because they believe that the cost of the supplements per person for whom institutionalization is being delayed is less than the states' costs under Medicaid for nursing home care. Indeed, because participating states fully fund SSI supplements, compared with only partial funding of nursing home care under Medicaid, they apparently believe the effects of service provision on delaying institutionalization to be substantial. These benefits may not be perceived strictly in terms of delayed institutionalization, however; most states also place a high value on the higher morale and life satisfaction of those who are able to continue to live in the community compared to those in nursing homes.

The foregoing demonstrates the logic of using savings from reduced Medicaid payments to finance the package of housing and supportive services. Such a system could evolve into one in which Medicaid monies are used to fund congregate housing or other housing/support-service combinations simply because it is universally assumed that such expenditures are more effective than additional payments for nursing home care. However, the foregoing also illustrates that the available information cannot support the careful estimates needed to make this case; indeed, the available evidence indicates that net savings may be impossible to achieve. To be able to move forward with a system based explicitly on this logic requires the development of much better data on the delay in reductions in institutionalization and other long-term-care costs for those associated with the best designed congregate housing and other germane systems. If this evidence is forthcoming, then the task would be to convince the states that funding such programs is in their interest.

There is another reason to analyze carefully the effect of supportive services on delayed institutionalization. Although there is broad agreement on the desirability of the benefits of higher life satisfaction to frail elders' remaining in the community, there is no good estimate of what these benefits cost. Documentation of the reduction in nursing home care costs associated with supportive housing would permit estimation of the costs of all other benefits as a residual. Government could then decide whether such benefits are worth the additional expenditures necessary for a widely available supportive housing program.

OTHER FEDERAL-STATE COOPERATIVE FUNDING

Under this model, the federal and state governments would recognize the existing deficits in the volume of supportive services being provided to frail elderly occupants of assisted housing and would agree on joint funding of the needed services. Services would be provided to occupants of assisted housing funded by both the federal and state governments. This model would continue the existing arrangement for many health and welfare programs (e.g., Medicaid and Aid to Families with Dependent Children).

The financial incentive for the state is its ability to leverage federal dollars with which to provide support services. The matching rate for the state contribution would be determined by Congress. State participation would depend in part on the matching rate. It is likely that some states would not participate, even if the rate were quite generous. This situation would be unfortunate because it would result in inequitable treatment of otherwise similar frail elderly depending on where they live, and some elders needing these services would continue going without them. Such inequities would parallel those already existing because of differences among states in providing funding for programs serving the elderly, including SSI supplements.

Although a wide range of techniques could be used to provide the services, some standardized elements would be required: a common method of impairment assessment and a common definition of eligibility for service receipt in terms of physical or mental impairment; common requirements for tailoring services provided to each recipient, in turn suggesting essential case management services; and common copayment requirements unless states are willing to cover the costs of lower-than-standard copayment rates. Some variation would also be good, in light of the wide variety of housing environments--ranging from specially designed projects for the elderly to scattered rental units of the Section 8 Existing program--in which services would be provided. The cost of services should be defined on a state-by-state basis, and modest variation in the range of services that could be provided may be useful. Likewise, in terms of actual service delivery mechanisms, the states could be free to choose from a variety of alternatives, ranging from use of capitated S/HMO systems where they exist to housing agencies' contracting with vendors for services or using their own staffs to deliver services.

Several options also exist for funding and management at the federal level:

1. The funds could be channeled through the Title III program (appropriately modified), with an explicit earmark for the use of the funds.
2. Funds could be appropriated to HUD for an expanded, more flexible conception of the CHSP.
3. Federal SSI supplements for this purpose could be funded, although some occupants of both federal and state assisted housing would not be income eligible for services.[4]
4. A wholly new funding program could be created in either HUD or the Department of Health and Human Services.

Almost regardless of the funding arrangement, there is a strong case for housing providers to receive subsidies for both housing assistance and support services from a single agency, even if the funds originate from several distinct sources. To serve those in assisted housing, we favor HUD, rather than state-level social service agencies, to unify funds and pay the housing providers. The department through its area offices has a well-established supervisory and financial relationship with the projects that should not be disrupted. On the other hand, state social service agencies have developed expertise on functional assessment and service delivery which HUD lacks; in cases not involving federal housing projects, the state social service agency should probably channel federal monies.

There are several arguments for a unified funding stream. Under this arrangement, HUD would have accurate knowledge of the funding situation at each project, which would permit it to exercise management oversight better. Currently, for example, state agencies responsible for their congregate housing programs and most federally funded elderly projects do now know the full cost of the services that participants receive. Such information would also enable HUD to speak more effectively for supportive housing programs. Further, unifying the funding stream would greatly simplify the process of securing services for housing providers (e.g., applying to and negotiating with multiple sponsors and reporting to each on different forms).

How would a unified funding system work when, for example, the federal and state governments jointly funded support services? Our idea is for the states to transfer the necessary funds to HUD for dispersal to the projects. Annually, HUD would estimate, based on program data, the number of frail elderly to receive subsidized supportive services and inform the states, who would in turn make the necessary payment to HUD, based on the matching rate. At the end of the year, there would be a reconciliation based on actual usage. If the federal funds were appropriated to another agency, a similar procedure would apply. The provider would deal with a single agency and receive payments from a single source--in this case, HUD.

An important question concerns whether the states in effect lose control of their funds by participating in this process. They need not. There are at least three ways for the states to have a powerful role in determining the content and administration of such a program:

1. The package of services to be provided would be decided jointly by the state and the federal government as part of the process for HUD and the states to commit funding for services. Because the states are paying for some of the services, some latitude could be possible.

2. Although HUD would have the primary oversight responsibility through the area office network, state or local social service agencies should fully participate with HUD in conducting management reviews. The state agencies would have primary responsibility for reviewing delivery of supportive services and recommending corrective actions where necessary; if projects were ultimately judged incapable of providing services competently, the state would have the right to withdraw services from the project. (But HUD/state action would be taken to help participants find other housing.) Results of management and financial

reviews conducted by HUD would be shared with the germane state agency.

3. An advisory group drawn from among participating states would be created to review proposed modifications in HUD regulations governing the program to ensure that the states' interests and views were fully considered in this process.

Ways could be developed to ensure that states "get credit" with clients for providing the services. Posters could be placed in projects, and copayment notices could contain a small statement that the costs of services are partly paid by the state, for example.

Chapter 7 presents a recommended course of action. The cost of this type of arrangement is discussed below.

THE COSTS OF SERVING THE AT-RISK POPULATION IN ASSISTED HOUSING

To address the question of how much supportive services would cost, as noted, data on the size of the at-risk population to be served and on the average costs of serving each person are necessary.

The proportion of over-65 residents of assisted housing who will require institutionalization within two years is 4.1 percent. (See chapter 2.) This estimate was made with the benefit of hindsight. A program designed to preempt institutionalization must serve those whom it identifies as potentially at risk, and this targeting can be as good only as the best available functional assessment procedure. None of the available measures is a good predictor of eventual institutionalization. (See chapter 2 for a description.) ADL measures seem to be the best, and they do help identify which elderly need assistance and in which areas. Only between 4.9 and 8.9 percent of elderly assisted renters have one or more ADL limitations requiring assistance. This statement means that between 75,000 and 135,000 frail elderly live in assisted housing. As noted earlier, this number is a reasonable

TABLE 6.3A   COMPARISON OF COSTS AND AVAILABLE FUNDING FOR SUPPORTIVE SERVICES
(Using a Lower-Bound Estimate of the Number of Frail Elderly in Assisted Housing)

State	Applicable SSBG/Title III Funds[a] (hundred $s)	Lower Bound Estimate of Frail Elderly in Assisted Housing[b]	At $650 per Person per Month				At $350 per Person per Month			
			Total Annual Service Cost (hundred $s)	Funds - Cost (hundred $s)	Cost as Percentage of Funds	Percent of Frail Served	Total Annual Service Cost (hundred $s)	Funds - Cost (hundred $s)	Cost as Percentage of Funds	Percent of Frail Served
ALABAMA	$ 27,144	889	$ 6,932	$ 20,211	26	100	$ 3,733	$ 23,411	14	100
ALASKA	7,121	56	437	6,684	6	100	235	6,885	3	100
ARIZONA	15,646	618	4,823	10,822	31	100	2,597	13,049	17	100
ARKANSAS	12,820	874	6,818	6,002	53	100	3,671	9,149	29	100
CALIFORNIA[c]	130,092	7,172	55,942	74,150	43	100	30,123	99,969	23	100
COLORADO	8,540	1,035	8,073	467	95	100	4,347	4,193	51	100
CONNECTICUT	17,861	1,518	11,843	6,017	66	100	6,377	11,484	36	100
DELAWARE	5,685	217	1,694	3,992	30	100	912	4,773	16	100
D.C.[c]	5,634	381	2,973	2,661	53	100	1,601	4,033	28	100
FLORIDA	61,028	2,744	21,401	39,628	35	100	11,523	49,505	19	100
GEORGIA	19,322	1,639	12,783	6,539	66	100	6,883	12,439	36	100
HAWAII	7,934	207	1,616	6,318	20	100	870	7,064	11	100
IDAHO	5,072	205	1,602	3,470	32	100	863	4,209	17	100
ILLINOIS	40,099	3,548	27,678	12,421	69	100	14,903	25,196	37	100
INDIANA[c]	29,424	1,542	12,024	17,400	41	100	6,474	22,949	22	100
IOWA	12,768	953	7,436	5,332	58	100	4,004	8,764	31	100
KANSAS	13,083	810	6,317	6,767	48	100	3,401	9,682	26	100
KENTUCKY[c]	20,133	1,333	10,397	9,736	52	100	5,598	14,534	28	100
LOUISIANA	35,962	989	7,714	28,248	21	100	4,154	31,809	12	100
MAINE	5,481	611	4,767	714	87	100	2,567	2,914	47	100
MARYLAND	20,507	1,470	11,468	9,039	56	100	6,175	14,332	30	100

State	Applicable SSBG/Title III Funds[a] (hundred $s)	Lower Bound Estimate of Frail Elderly in Assisted Housing[b]	At $650 per Person per Month				At $350 per Person per Month			
			Total Annual Service Cost (hundred $s)	Funds - Cost (hundred $s)	Cost as Percentage of Funds	Percent of Frail Served	Total Annual Service Cost (hundred $s)	Funds - Cost (hundred $s)	Cost as Percentage of Funds	Percent of Frail Served
MASSACHUSETTS	21,987	3,283	25,610	(3,622)	116	86	13,790	8,198	63	100
MICHIGAN	56,693	3,088	24,088	32,605	42	100	12,970	43,722	23	100
MINNESOTA[c]	22,890	2,309	18,011	4,880	79	100	9,698	13,192	42	100
MISSISSIPPI	12,279	487	3,801	8,478	31	100	2,046	10,232	17	100
MISSOURI	30,377	1,840	14,355	16,021	47	100	7,730	22,647	25	100
MONTANA	4,375	308	2,405	1,970	55	100	1,295	3,080	30	100
NEBRASKA	15,309	713	5,559	9,750	36	100	2,993	12,315	20	100
NEVADA[c]	6,252	209	1,627	4,625	26	100	876	5,376	14	100
NEW HAMPSHIRE	8,836	501	3,911	4,924	44	100	2,106	6,730	24	100
NEW JERSEY	37,971	2,986	23,293	14,677	61	100	12,542	25,428	33	100
NEW MEXICO	8,242	259	2,017	6,225	24	100	1,086	7,156	13	100
NEW YORK	101,469	6,070	47,349	54,120	47	100	25,496	75,973	25	100
NORTH CAROLINA	35,266	1,443	11,257	24,009	32	100	6,062	29,204	17	100
NORTH DAKOTA[c]	5,771	278	2,165	3,606	38	100	1,166	4,605	20	100
OHIO	97,782	3,897	30,400	67,382	31	100	16,369	81,412	17	100
OKLAHOMA	14,008	795	6,204	7,805	44	100	3,340	10,668	24	100
OREGON	12,895	895	6,979	5,916	54	100	3,758	9,137	29	100
PENNSYLVANIA	54,511	4,596	35,846	18,665	66	100	19,302	35,209	35	100
RHODE ISLAND	7,168	1,066	8,316	(1,148)	116	86	4,478	2,690	62	100
SOUTH CAROLINA	14,513	553	4,313	10,201	30	100	2,322	12,191	16	100
SOUTH DAKOTA	5,978	305	2,375	3,603	40	100	1,279	4,699	21	100
TENNESSEE	25,741	1,563	12,193	13,548	47	100	6,566	19,175	26	100
TEXAS	97,798	2,828	22,062	75,736	23	100	11,879	85,918	12	100
UTAH	5,248	270	2,105	3,143	40	100	1,133	4,114	22	100

State	Applicable SSBG/Title III Funds[a] (hundred $s)	Lower Bound Estimate of Frail Elderly in Assisted Housing[b]	At $650 per Person per Month				At $350 per Person per Month			
			Total Annual Service Cost (hundred $s)	Funds - Cost (hundred $s)	Cost as Percentage of Funds	Percent of Frail Served	Total Annual Service Cost (hundred $s)	Funds - Cost (hundred $s)	Cost as Percentage of Funds	Percent of Frail Served
VERMONT	4,512	221	1,725	2,787	38	100	929	3,583	21	100
VIRGINIA	29,310	1,053	8,210	21,100	28	100	4,421	24,889	15	100
WASHINGTON	26,677	1,454	11,344	15,333	43	100	6,109	20,569	23	100
WEST VIRGINIA	12,439	696	5,429	7,010	44	100	2,294	9,516	24	100
WISCONSIN	19,696	2,097	16,359	3,336	83	100	8,809	10,887	45	100
WYOMING	6,047	122	955	5,092	16	100	514	5,533	9	100
TOTAL	$1,303,397	75,000	$585,000	$718,397	45%	100%	$315,000	$988,397	24%	100%

Notes: Costs and funds in 1987 U.S. dollars. Parentheses signify negative numbers (i.e., inadequate funds). Assumes applicable SSBG/Title III funds only are expended, with no federal matching.

a. Includes the portion of SSBG funds currently being used by each state for elderly services (from Gaberlavage, 1987) and Title III B and C funds (from AoA program data). Funds are "available" only to the extent that the states are willing to redirect them to serving the elderly assisted housing population, thus sacrificing or funding alternate funding for some existing programs.

b. The number of people over 65 in assisted housing with one or more ADLS (see table 2.3) distributed by state, based on the distribution of elderly 202 and public housing units (from 1988 HUD program data provided by Joyce Ann Bassett and Eva Lance).

c. Percentage of SSBG funds allocated to elderly services unknown--national average (18.1 percent) assumed.

TABLE 6.3B   COMPARISON OF COSTS AND AVAILABLE FUNDING FOR SUPPORTIVE SERVICES
(Using an Upper-Bound Estimate of the Number of Frail Elderly in Assisted Housing)

State	Applicable SSBG/Title III Funds[a] (hundred $s)	Upper Bound Estimate of Frail Elderly in Assisted Housing[b]	At $650 per Person per Month				At $350 per Person per Month			
			Total Annual Service Cost (hundred $s)	Funds - Cost (hundred $s)	Cost as Percentage of Funds	Percent of Frail Served	Total Annual Service Cost (hundred $s)	Funds - Cost (hundred $s)	Cost as Percentage of Funds	Percent of Frail Served
ALABAMA	$ 27,144	1,600	$ 12,478	$ 14,666	46	100	$ 6,719	$ 20,425	25	100
ALASKA	7,121	101	787	6,334	11	100	424	6,697	6	100
ARIZONA	15,646	1,113	8,682	6,964	55	100	4,675	10,971	30	100
ARKANSAS	12,820	1,573	12,272	548	96	100	6,608	6,212	52	100
CALIFORNIA[c]	130,092	12,910	100,696	29,396	77	100	54,221	75,871	42	100
COLORADO	8,540	1,863	14,532	(5,992)	170	59	7,825	715	92	100
CONNECTICUT	17,861	2,733	21,318	(3,457)	119	84	11,479	6,382	64	100
DELAWARE	5,685	391	3,049	2,637	54	100	1,642	4,044	29	100
D.C.[c]	5,634	686	5,351	283	95	100	2,881	2,753	51	100
FLORIDA	61,028	4,939	38,521	22,507	63	100	20,742	40,286	34	100
GEORGIA	19,322	2,950	23,009	3,687	119	84	12,390	6,933	64	100
HAWAII	7,934	373	2,909	5,025	37	100	1,566	6,368	20	100
IDAHO	5,072	370	2,884	2,189	57	100	1,553	3,520	31	100
ILLINOIS	40,099	6,387	49,820	(9,721)	124	80	26,826	13,273	67	100
INDIANA[c]	29,424	2,775	21,643	7,781	74	100	11,654	17,770	40	100
IOWA	12,768	1,716	13,385	(617)	105	95	7,207	5,561	56	100
KANSAS	13,083	1,458	11,370	1,714	87	100	6,122	6,961	47	100
KENTUCKY[c]	20,133	2,399	18,715	1,418	93	100	10,077	10,056	50	100
LOUISIANA	35,962	1,780	13,886	22,077	39	100	7,477	28,486	21	100
MAINE	5,481	1,100	8,580	(3,099)	157	64	4,620	861	84	100
MARYLAND	20,507	2,647	20,643	(136)	101	99	11,115	9,391	54	100

State	Applicable SSBG/Title III Funds[a] (hundred $s)	Lower Bound Estimate of Frail Elderly in Assisted Housing[b]	At $650 per Person per Month				At $350 per Person per Month			
			Total Annual Service Cost (hundred $s)	Funds - Cost (hundred $s)	Cost as Percentage of Funds	Percent of Frail Served	Total Annual Service Cost (hundred $s)	Funds - Cost (hundred $s)	Cost as Percentage of Funds	Percent of Frail Served
MASSACHUSETTS	21,987	5,910	46,097	(24,110)	210	48	24,822	(2,834)	113	89
MICHIGAN	56,693	5,559	43,358	13,335	76	100	23,347	33,346	41	100
MINNESOTA[c]	22,890	4,156	32,419	(9,529)	142	71	17,456	5,434	76	100
MISSISSIPPI	12,279	877	6,841	5,438	56	100	3,684	8,595	30	100
MISSOURI	30,377	3,313	25,839	4,537	85	100	13,913	16,463	46	100
MONTANA	4,375	555	4,329	46	99	100	2,331	2,044	53	100
NEBRASKA	15,309	1,283	10,006	5,302	65	100	5,388	9,921	35	100
NEVADA[c]	6,252	375	2,929	3,324	47	100	1,577	4,675	25	100
NEW HAMPSHIRE	8,836	903	7,041	1,795	80	100	3,791	5,045	43	100
NEW JERSEY	37,971	5,375	41,928	(3,957)	110	91	22,576	15,394	59	100
NEW MEXICO	8,242	465	3,630	4,612	44	100	1,955	6,288	24	100
NEW YORK	101,469	10,927	85,228	16,241	84	100	45,892	55,577	45	100
NORTH CAROLINA	35,266	2,598	20,263	15,003	57	100	10,991	24,355	31	100
NORTH DAKOTA[c]	5,771	500	3,897	1,874	68	100	2,098	3,673	36	100
OHIO	97,782	7,015	54,720	43,062	56	100	29,465	68,317	30	100
OKLAHOMA	14,008	1,432	11,166	2,842	80	100	6,013	7,996	43	100
OREGON	12,895	1,611	12,563	332	97	100	6,765	6,131	52	100
PENNSYLVANIA	54,511	8,272	64,523	(10,012)	118	84	34,743	19,768	64	89
RHODE ISLAND	7,168	1,919	14,969	(7,800)	209	48	8,060	(892)	112	100
SOUTH CAROLINA	14,513	995	7,763	6,751	53	100	4,180	10,333	29	100
SOUTH DAKOTA	5,978	548	4,275	1,703	72	100	2,302	3,676	39	100
TENNESSEE	25,741	2,814	21,948	3,793	85	100	11,818	13,923	46	100
TEXAS	97,798	5,091	39,711	58,087	41	100	21,383	76,415	22	100
UTAH	5,248	486	3,788	1,459	72	100	2,040	3,208	39	100

State	Applicable SSBG/Title III Funds[a] (hundred $s)	Lower Bound Estimate of Frail Elderly in Assisted Housing[b]	At $650 per Person per Month				At $350 per Person per Month			
			Total Annual Service Cost (hundred $s)	Funds - Cost (hundred $s)	Cost as Percentage of Funds	Percent of Frail Served	Total Annual Service Cost (hundred $s)	Funds - Cost (hundred $s)	Cost as Percentage of Funds	Percent of Frail Served
VERMONT	4,512	398	3,105	1,407	69	100	1,672	2,840	37	100
VIRGINIA	29,310	1,895	14,777	14,533	50	100	7,957	21,353	27	100
WASHINGTON	26,677	2,618	20,420	6,257	77	100	10,995	15,682	41	100
WEST VIRGINIA	12,439	1,253	9,773	2,667	79	100	5,262	7,177	42	100
WISCONSIN	19,696	3,775	29,447	9,751	150	67	15,856	3,840	81	100
WYOMING	6,047	220	1,719	4,328	28	100	926	5,121	15	100
TOTAL	$1,303,397	135,000	$1,053,000	$250,397	81%	100%	$567,000	$736,397	44%	100%

Note: Costs and funds in 1987 dollars. Parentheses signify negative numbers (i.e., inadequate funds).
Assumes applicable SSBG/Title III funds only are expended, with no federal matching.

a. Includes the portion of SSBG funds currently being used by each state for elderly services (from Gaberlavage, 1987) and Title III B and C funds (from AoA program data). Funds are "available" only to the extent that the states are willing to redirect them to serving the elderly assisted housing population, thus sacrificing or funding alternate funding for some existing programs.

b. The number of people over 65 in assisted housing with one or more ADLS (see table 2.3) distributed by state, based on the distribution of elderly 202 and public housing units (from 1988 HUD program data provided by Joyce Ann Bassett and Eva Lance).

c. Percentage of SSBG funds allocated to elderly services unknown—national average (18.1 percent) assumed.

approximation of those that a nationally administered supportive services program targeted on individuals with functional impairments would need to serve; it does not seem to be beyond the capacity of government help.[5]

Table 6.3 shows the distribution of these frail assisted housing residents by state.[6] The table shows four estimates: for each of the upper and lower estimates of the number of frail elderly, the upper and lower monthly cost estimates of providing supportive services are given. Table 6.3A is for an estimated 75,000 frail elderly, table 6.3B for 135,000 frail elderly.

The monthly cost estimates shown are based on existing federal and state congregate services programs; they give upper and lower bounds for providing a range of nonmedical support services, including one hot meal per day.[7] CHSP and various comparable (but generally more expensive) state programs were examined. These costs (in 1987 dollars), ranging from $350 to $650 per person per month, cluster toward the lower figure. Costs vary with location, the type of service the provider used, the intensity of services provided, and the success of targeting. These last two factors are inversely related--the frailer the resident served, the greater the level and per capita cost of needed services.

Table 6.3 shows that, nationally, it would cost between $315 million and $585 million annually to serve an assisted elderly population of 75,000 and between $736 million and $1,053 million to serve 135,000. Under a federal-state funding program like that discussed in the last section, the federal government would be appropriating additional monies to provide supportive services. The tabulation in table 6.4 shows what federal funding would be in 1987 under assumptions about the population served, the share of funding provided by the federal government, the cost per month of services, and the share of service costs paid for by recipients (15 percent). Depending on the parameters employed, additional annual federal appropriations would be from $134 to $537 million. For a program with a 50 percent sharing rate, a $350 monthly cost of support services (like that for CHSP) to serve 135,000 frail elders (the midpoint of the range of estimates) would cost the federal government $241 million, in addition to its housing subsidies.

These are large numbers. However, they substantially overstate the actual increase in expenditures for several reasons. First, there would be some reduction in Medicaid expenditures from both reduced nursing home placements and lower use of acute care facilities. Second, supportive services provided in an integrated supportive housing program would displace some subsidized services previously received by participants. And, third, there should be some gains in the degree of service tailoring that would also cut costs.

Table 6.3 also lists the applicable federal funds each state has available to it from the SSBG and Title III programs that could be directed to a supportive service program for assisted housing. The table shows a high and a low estimate of the cost of providing services to the two estimated frail populations in order to gauge the adequacy of funding available to the states.[8] States, of course, would have to be willing to redirect these "available" funds to support service programs aimed at serving the assisted housing population. In other words, to say for a particular state that available funds are adequate to cover the need is not to deny that other current programs would have to be sacrificed or otherwise financed.

About $1.3 billion is available to the states for elderly services from the aforementioned federal sources; 24-45 percent of it would suffice to pay for the services needed for a beneficiary population of 75,000, depending on their costs. For 135,000 recipients, 44-81 percent of these funds would be required. If one assumes that the federal government would be contributing at least half the total cost under arrangements considered here, then a proportionately smaller share of available funds would be required for the states' contributions.

As expected, there is a good deal of variation in the states' ability to use these "available funds" to fund support services for frail elders in assisted housing without seriously impinging on present uses of the funds. Table 6.5 shows the number of states that would have to devote various shares of the available funds under two estimates of the monthly service costs and of the population to be served. These levels-of-effort figures all exclude any federal payments or beneficiary copayments for the

TABLE 6.4   ANNUAL FEDERAL FUNDING TO SERVE ALL
THE FRAIL ELDERLY IN GOVERNMENT-
ASSISTED HOUSING UNDER ALTERNATIVE
RATES AND COST ASSUMPTIONS, 1987

Frail Population	Federal Funding Share (percentage)	Cost per Month of Services (million dollars)	
		$650	$350
75,000	50	249	134
	60	298	160
135,000	50	447	241
	60	537	289

Note: Federal cost reduced by assuming that copayments by
recipients cover 15 percent of total cost.

TABLE 6.5   ESTIMATED NUMBER OF STATES NEEDING TO
SPEND SELECTED PERCENTAGES OF
"AVAILABLE FUNDS" FOR SUPPORT SERVICES
TO THE FRAIL ELDERLY IN GOVERNMENT
ASSISTED HOUSING

Population	Percentage of Available Funds	Cost of Services per Month (mill. $)	
		$650	$350
75,000	> 100	2	20
	70-100	4	0
	0-10	20	45
135,000	> 100	13	1
	90-100	16	4
	0-40	3	23

Note: Assumes no federal payments and no beneficiary
copayments.

services (i.e., in effect, the figures show the case of full funding by the states).

For the high estimate 13 states would have to spend more than 100 percent and another 16 states 70-100 percent of the "available funds" to provide these services. Only three states would be spending less than 40 percent of their available funds. Even after allowing for a 50 percent federal match, which cuts the states' level of effort in half, these figures suggest a substantial diversion of funds away from current activities. For the low estimate no state would spend as much as 70 percent of its available funds on these services; and the vast majority would spend less than 40 percent.

Possibly the most intriguing aspect of the patterns just reviewed is the variation among states within a particular option. The reason why some states have to devote such a large share of available funds compared to others is that they have some combination of the following attributes: a large population of elderly people in assisted housing; they have decided to devote a small share of SSBG funds to elderly services; and/or they have a relatively small total elderly population, which reduces the monies received under OAA Title III. The first of these factors increases costs and the other two cut available revenues. Note, however, that a state that would have to devote a large share of its available funds to meet these expenditures is not necessarily one with low overall expenditures on the elderly; the state may be spending substantial amounts of its own funds for this purpose.

Overall, states could generally meet the funding requirements of supportive services using SSBG and Title III funds without much difficulty, assuming a reasonable federal matching rate. If the point of reference is the "average" case--a 50 percent federal matching rate, 105,000 beneficiaries--then, on average, the states would have to use between 17 and 31 percent of their available SSBG and Title III funds to serve the population under study, depending on the monthly cost of services ($350 to $650). In either case, to use the available funds to pay for support services for the frail elderly would require difficult and possibly explicit political choices to reallocate assistance among groups of their citizens.

CONCLUDING COMMENT

This chapter presents three alternative models of federal-state cooperation in providing supportive services to the frail elderly living in federal assisted housing. The first two models are limited, either in concept or concrete supporting information, which may argue against immediate adoption.

The model of "federal housing assistance and state supportive services" would not help those frail elderly already living in assisted housing except to the extent that the occupants were shifted to newly created or rehabilitated projects. Hence, additional sources of supportive services are required to complement the creation of the new units earmarked for the frail elderly.

The model of "joint federal-state funding from Medicaid savings" is limited by lack of data on the ability of well-designed supportive service programs to delay institutionalization. Although it is not an absolute requirement that the supportive services be demonstrated to produce a net savings in Medicaid funds from lower institutionalization or other long-term-care costs, some reliable data are necessary for states and the federal government to judge whether the other benefits from delayed institutionalization--higher morale and greater life satisfaction of the elderly--more than compensate for any greater cost that provision of supportive services entails.

The model of "other joint federal-state funding of supportive services" offers many possibilities and options. But it appears possible that a workable funding program could be quickly fashioned.

Regardless of the model chosen or the combinations of funding resources used, our estimates indicate that the total annual cost of including the estimated 105,000 elderly assisted housing residents needing personal assistance with one or more ADL limitations in a supportive service program is between $441 million and $819 million. Although this money would essentially go to the creation of a new program, the program could be expected to substitute significantly for some other governmental spending (e.g., Medicaid, Medicare, some support services already being provided) and to redirect or use some existing applicable funds (e.g., Title III, SSBG) so that the net additional cost would be considerably less. Some system of tenant copayments and federal matching or specialization could also serve to share the burden more fairly among recipients, states, and the federal government.

In short, the costs seem not to be prohibitive, but the information does not exist to support endorsement of any specific approach at this time. One approach may have to be selected and implemented in the near term because of the urgency of helping the frail elderly in assisted housing. To prepare for this eventuality, chapter 7 indicates how the country might proceed. In any case, the years ahead should be the setting for a great deal of experimentation and analysis of alternatives so that the superior options can be identified before the needs of the much larger cohorts of frail elderly after the turn of the century must be addressed.

Notes, chapter 6

1.   Obviously, state appropriations for this purpose are a possibility. However, if the objective is for these services to be available in all states (for equity), relying on each state legislature appropriating the necessary funds (and possibly taking additional authorization action) may not be prudent.

2.   Most elderly households in assisted housing are Medicaid-eligible, and the savings to Medicaid would be larger than the additional costs of the supportive services expenditures.

2a. The cost of housing services and housing subsidies under the CHSP were derived under the following assumptions: (a) the income of the elderly receiving this assistance was the same as that of all elderly receiving housing assistance; and, (b) the cost of housing services in public housing and section 202 projects was the same as the average outlays under the entire Section 8 program. Under these assumptions, total rent in 1985 was $430 per month and federal outlays were $274 per month. The full monthly cost of services, including $340 per month for supportive services (both those paid for by CHSP and matching services provided by the facility), was $770. (The cost of supportive services is from program data. Income data come from Current Population Survey data reported in U.S. Bureau of the Census (1985); note these are not the same income data as in table 2.3. Section 8 outlays are from HUD budget documents.)

3. The "60 percent of the time" figure is computed as the reciprocal of the "break-even" or cost-neutral targeting rate (i.e., 1/1.65) used in table 6.2. At a targeting rate of 80 percent of break-even, a person in supportive housing would have to be kept out of the institution 48 percent of the time (.8/1.65).

4.   For more on this option, see Center for the Study of Social Policy (1988).

5.   The proportion of elderly in assisted housing who are frail--currently somewhat less than among all elderly renters-- might be expected to rise somewhat as an established service program permitted frailer persons to remain in their assisted unit or to leave an institution.

6.   The number of over-65 persons with one or more ADL limitations (from chapter 2), distributed by state, is based on the distribution of elderly-occupied Sections 8, 202, and 236 and public housing units by state (from 1988 HUD program data). The proportion of frail is assumed to be constant across all states.

7.   Costs were calculated by factoring out housing and meal costs from overall estimates of total costs (including program expenditures, tenant fees, and other governmental assistance). An average cost of $100 per month was then added to each to cover a standard daily hot meal.

8.   Applicable funds currently available to the states are calculated to include Older Americans Act (OAA) Title III funds for supportive and nutrition services (Title III B and C, from Administration on Aging program data) and the portion of SSBG funds currently devoted to elderly services (Gaberlavage 1987).

RECOMMENDATIONS

Today there are an estimated 105,000 elderly occupants of assisted housing (the midpoint of a 95 percent confidence interval of 75,000 to 135,000) who likely need supportive services to help them continue living independent, full lives. This is a number that federal and state governments together could assist with less than $1 billion in new or reallocated resources. The net expenditures would be even less after a tally of reductions in institutional care and other costs incurred from not having these services in place.

At the same time, policymakers must be aware that this number will grow over the years ahead. Under simple assumptions an increase of about 35,000 in the number of frail elderly in assisted housing having a limitation in at least one ADL requiring personal assistance between 1988 and 2000 is estimated. This is a one-third increase over the current population.[1] Of course, after 2010 when the baby-boom cohort reaches retirement, this growth could accelerate, depending on the growth in assisted housing and other factors. Moreover, making supportive services available in assisted housing may cause those needing such services to apply for assisted housing in disproportionate numbers or to remain there longer as their health deteriorates and thus raise the numbers even further. All cost figures should be adjusted proportionately for these increases to obtain cost estimates for future years (in constant dollars).

This chapter presents recommendations on how to provide supportive services to this population. It builds directly on the pieces of information developed in the previous chapters, and it is organized in two parts. The first deals with what services to provide and how to organize their provision. The second section addresses the question of how to fund them.

A major theme of the recommendations is that the next decade is an opportunity for the United States to experiment boldly and widely to identify cost-effective ways of assisting the frail elderly to continue active lives in the community. The problems of insufficient assistance with key activities of daily living of this population in assisted housing are similar to those of other frail elderly, and federal and state governments--based on their mutual interests in aiding this population and reducing long-term-care expenditures--can take the lead in designing effective packages of housing and support services. Hence, the recommendations focus on exploring alternatives rather than putting forward a single approach that might not be defensible when new information is developed.

PROVISION OF SERVICES

An effective system of delivering supportive services to the frail elderly requires several key elements, including targeting services on those who need them and tailoring them. The next several paragraphs provide the recommendations on these elements based on what the project team perceives to be "best practices" in the federal and state programs reviewed. The recommendations on congressional action to foster the development of several promising delivery systems follow.

Selection of those elderly to receive supportive services is clearly the starting point for designing a system of service delivery. The first imperative is for the development of better operational indicators of the risk of institutionalization for frail elders. Without these measures the targeting of services will be difficult and program efficiency reduced.

In terms of the minimum degree of frailty required for admittance, a reasonable standard based on available indicators is for the presence of a limitation with at least one activity of daily living severe enough to require personal assistance and one or more instrumental activity of daily living limitations. At least as important as the standard itself, however, is its correct and consistent interpretation. "Limitation in movement" encompasses a wide range of conditions, and those evaluating prospective participants must have clear guidance on the degree of impairment that constitutes sufficient severity to warrant admission. In this regard, use of a centralized screening system at the local level, rather than staff at each project conducting their own assessments, is certainly advisable (and better documentation of current practices could well make it warranted), as are national guidelines on conducting assessments. In addition, the practice in Massachusetts of one assessment session taking place in the applicant's home to observe the types of adaptations that have been made in response to the disability seems advisable.

Case management to ensure careful tailoring of services to the needs of each participant is also essential. The combination of case management and tailoring is central to any cost-containment effort and to assisting the frail person effectively. Client evaluation and service prescription should be repeated at least annually after admission into the program. Proper case management requires a well-qualified (either by credentialed skills or experience) manager at each project or per specified number of recipients in scattered-site housing.

The services package should contain one congregate meal per day, case management, housekeeping and periodic chore services, personal care, laundry assistance, and transportation services. Consistent with tailoring, mandatory items should be sharply restricted; the prime candidate for requirement is one congregate meal per day in housing projects (but not necessarily in scattered-site housing) because of the economies of scale in food preparation. Further, for those needing a higher level of care than can be provided by congregate services, more routine arrangements should be established between the Department of Housing and Urban Development (HUD) and state Medicaid offices for transferring people into the Medicaid waiver programs supporting the higher level of assistance.

In terms of actual service provision, providing cash payments to the housing project or household with which to purchase services from vendors or to deliver them directly is superior to the housing project brokering in-kind services from several sources funded directly by state agencies. Providing the payments to the housing project manager or household allows an ability to achieve close tailoring of services not otherwise possible, and it dramatically simplifies management and coordination. To implement the "cash budget" approach may require stronger qualifications and training for the on-site case managers.

With regard to tailoring services through use of a cash budget, various "maintenance of effort" requirements imposed on projects by congregate programs may not be wise. They press the facility to continue acquiring services for occupants that may not be truly necessary, thereby pushing program costs upward while having little impact on such key outcomes as delaying institutionalization. Proponents of "maintenance of effort" requirements believe that they hold down the cost of a particular program, regardless of the impact on total costs. The solution clearly is in a simplified integrated service delivery system. Most of these requirements are legislatively mandated and Congress would have to act to change them.

Further, agency oversight is essential for ensuring quality of services, targeting, and administration. Such oversight will become more important as the shift to the housing project's having greater responsibility for service provision under the "cash budget" arrangement is implemented. Currently, financial oversight of service provision is vastly complicated (or rendered impossible) by the multiple sources of in-kind services.

There is no reason why the "best practices" just enumerated could not be incorporated into any of the systems discussed in the previous chapters: federal and state congregate housing programs, the Congregate Housing Certificate Program (CHCP), the social/health maintenance organizations (S/HMOs), the Housing and Support Services Certificate Program (HSSCP), and the Supplemental Security Income (SSI) congregate care supplement. At the same time, many of the currently operating models would require very significant revisions to be consistent with these practices. Several programs now embody questionable incentives and few cost controls.

As argued earlier, now is the time for frank experimentation (and evaluation) as a way for identifying cost-

effective models of housing with supportive services to su.
the frail elderly in the community. To this end, fouⁱ
recommendations are made:

1. If congress continues funding for the Congregate
Housing Services Program (CHSP), it might be used as
a laboratory for analyzing the effects of program
improvements. The CHSP should be altered to
conform with the "best practices" outlined above.
Moreover, it seems reasonable that if a joint state-
federal financing model is adopted for providing
assistance to additional households, it should be
applied to CHSP as well.

2. Demonstrate the HSSCP in several cities for a
period of 5-10 years. This approach holds great
promise for assisting frail elders in units assisted with
Section 8 and housing vouchers and for those living in
housing projects. The discipline of providing services
within the resources provided by the certificate may
achieve substantial efficiencies.

Considerable latitude should be given to
participating local administering agencies in the early
years in the ways they elect to deliver services (e.g.,
subcontracting for the entire program, alternative
arrangements with state and local social service
agencies); based on experience, superior alternatives
should be identified.

3. Active, intense experimentation with capitated
programs should be continued. HUD, working with
the Health Care Financing Administration, should
enroll all the elderly in assisted housing in a
community in a S/HMO for a demonstration period of
5-10 years. This would provide an excellent test of
acceptance by assisted housing occupants and the
efficacy of the incentives in capitated systems for
achieving better tailoring and case management, which
should lead to lower costs and greater delays in
institutionalization. The best candidate S/HMO may
be the Kaiser Permanente program in Portland,
Oregon. (Residents in existing congregate projects

might be excluded, in part to use these projects as a control group.)

4. Demonstrate the Congregate Housing Certificate Program model in a couple cities to evaluate its cost containment and service responsiveness attributes that should come from the cost limits imposed by the Augmented Fair Market Rents and competition among projects. The demonstration would have to involve enough projects to make competition meaningful and would have to be staged for a long enough time (7-10 years) to induce private housing suppliers to participate. Although CHCP may be of limited use in serving the current population of frail elders in assisted housing, it is recommended for a demonstration on the basis of what may be learned for future program design.

More analysis of the possibilities of the SSI supplements for funding supportive services in assisted housing also appears warranted in light of New York's successful use of this model. In several respects, including cost limits, it resembles CHCP.

The recommendations call for relatively long demonstration periods, ranging from 5 to 10 years. In part, they are needed to induce private suppliers to participate. At least as important, however, the long demonstration period provides the opportunity for an initial evaluation, program adjustment, and subsequent evaluation (i.e., the possibility of measuring improvements made in program performance based on early findings). This strategy, which provides both short-term results and a better long-term program, is seen as much superior to a brief one-time demonstration-evaluation period, such as that employed in the evaluation of the CHSP.

FUNDING SYSTEMS

Joint funding by the federal and state governments of supportive services in assisted housing makes sense because income maintenance and health care responsibilities have traditionally been shared by the two levels of government and because the savings in other long-term-care costs from providing such services will accrue to both levels. Before turning to funding sources, we should highlight several lessons about how to organize payments for services to projects and from participants.

In terms of payments to the housing provider for support services, reasons for giving providers cash with which to purchase or provide directly the services required by project occupants have been discussed. A related point is that housing providers should receive funds from a single agency, even when the funds originate in several distinct sources, as they would in several models of federal-state funding cooperation described in chapter 6. For those in federally assisted housing, we think the agency should be HUD. Under this arrangement, HUD area offices would have accurate knowledge of the funding situation of each project, permitting it to exercise management oversight better and enabling it to speak more effectively for supportive housing programs. Unifying the funding stream would also greatly simplify the fundraising and reporting tasks of the housing providers. In other situations the funds should flow through state social service agencies because of their greater expertise in client assessment and delivery of support services.

Payments from participants for services (i.e., copayments) are essential not only to offset program costs but also to help contain service use. As noted in the previous chapters, use of copayments is widespread, although in some programs they constitute only token amounts. Such payments should be large enough to help achieve the objectives for having them. In addition, they should be related to the quantity of services a participant receives to the extent possible (i.e., in cases of very low-income households, the ability to impose copayments is restricted by leaving them with sufficient income for life necessities).

Among the three models of joint federal-state funding presented in chapter 6, for reasons noted there, it is difficult to recommend one for immediate full-scale implementation. The "specialization model," in which the federal government would fund incremental housing units and the states would commit themselves to funding supportive services for at least 10 years, is not discussed further here for two reasons. It focuses on additional units and more participant frail households, whereas it is the existing population of frail persons in assisted housing that is of primary concern here. In addition, there is little need to experiment with this model because its individual components exist in other systems.

To be able to recommend the model that finances supportive services from Medicaid savings, we need more definitive information on the cost-effectiveness of the provision of these services in assisted housing in delaying institutional placement. Because of the limited number of nursing home beds in many states in recent years, a comprehensive evaluation would be difficult to execute, given the need to take account of the extra costs in acute and other care provided to those who remain in the community only because of excess nursing home demand.[2] To some extent, this problem of restricted nursing home access was present in the channeling demonstration, thereby limiting the extent to which care in the community substituted for nursing home care (Kemper 1988). In light of the current situation, the recommendation is for HUD and the Health Care Financing Administration together to evaluate the effectiveness of the newest revision of the CHSP and possibly one or two state programs that have strong targeting and tailoring components. As suggested earlier, one of the important products of such evaluations would be an estimate of the cost (net of any reductions in Medicaid expenditures for nursing home care) of achieving the benefits of improved morale and life satisfaction by residents of supportive housing.

In the next several years, the more general model of "joint federal-state funding" of supportive services should be pursued. The supportive services for the Housing and Support

Services Certificate Program, the payments of the insurance premiums for the S/HMO demonstration, and the CHCP demonstration would all be jointly funded. Congress could establish a new program and appropriate the necessary monies for the federal payments. The law would establish the state-federal matching rate, attempting to ensure substantial, if not universal, participation by the states.

Participating states would have to commit funding from reliable sources for a minimum of 10 years. "State sources" would include funds from the Social Services Block Grant program and Title III of the Older Americans Act, assuming that Congress makes the necessary legislative changes to permit such commitments; in using these sources, states would have to guarantee funding from general revenues in the event that the specified federal funding were reduced or discontinued.[3] Alternatively, and possibly more likely, states could commit state funds to this program. Consistent with other recommendations made here, federal appropriations might be made to the HUD budget because the programs under consideration are restricted to those in assisted housing units, although other appropriation vehicles are certainly possible. State funds would be channeled through HUD to obtain the full advantage of single-source financing noted above.

The next 15 years will be a critical time for the country to learn to care for its burgeoning population of frail elderly at an affordable cost. Part of the challenge is to turn away from strictly medically oriented approaches to address the problems of the lower-income frail elderly and to perceive housing combined with limited supportive services as a clearly appropriate alternative in many instances. The recommendations made above build on the limited information available and will, if accepted, generate vastly expanded experience on which to design the key component in the future long-term-care system that uses assisted housing as an integral element.

Notes, chapter 7

1.   We have assumed that the growth of the number of frail elderly having at least one limitation in an activity of daily living and at least one instrumental activity of daily living which require personal assistance depends primarily on the number of elderly in assisted housing. Based on discussions with staff at the Department of Housing and Urban Development, we assume that there will be 100,000 households added on net to the federal assisted housing roles between 1988 and the year 2000, or a total of 1.2 million units in total. If we assume that the elderly continue to be about 42 percent of program participants (which seems reasonable since HUD estimates they are about this share of both project-based and voucher recipients) and that those at risk of institutionalization remain the same share of all elderly as is the case currently, then in the year 2000 some 35,000 additional elderly would be served by a program providing support services to all those judged to require them, according to the definition used here. This figure could understate the increase in the number of at-risk elderly, if there is a disproportionately large cohort of housing assistance recipients in the 55 to 70 age group now, which remains in assisted housing and which more than replaces the current cohort of older, frail persons now in assisted housing. It would also understate the number to be served if the elderly constituted an even larger share of those entering the rolls of those receiving assistance or if the incidence of frailty increased. The latter point can be discounted, since there is no strong evidence of increasing morbidity among the elderly despite increases in longevity, although the topic is hotly debated in the literature.

2. One way around this problem is to identify areas of the country in which there is an adequate supply of nursing home beds and use these areas in the evaluation.

3. Commitment of anticipated funding from annual congressional appropriations to make bond payments is

permitted under the Section 108 provisions of the Community Development Block Grant (CDBG) program. The fallback position is that localities will make payments from general revenues if CDBG funding does not materialize.

APPENDICES

Appendix A
PROCEDURES FOR IMPUTING ASSISTED HOUSING
VARIABLES FROM THE 1978 AHS TO THE 1982-84 LTC

The 1982-84 National Long-Term Care Survey (LTC) contains a number of indicators of housing attributes, but not a measure of whether the sample person lives in government-assisted housing. This key variable must, therefore, be imputed from another data base, namely, the 1978 American Housing Survey (AHS). The 1978 AHS was used instead of a more recent AHS because only in the 1978 version of this national survey were sample households asked about health conditions and functional limitations; these items allow us to link the two surveys. Two primary activities were required to attach the government-assisted housing indicator from the AHS LTC: preparing an AHS data file suitable for the linkage and statistically imputing the value of this indicator from the AHS to the LTC. Each of these activities is described in turn.

PREPARING THE AHS DATA

The first step in this activity was to identify households in the AHS that included at least one person age 65 or older. This extract contained 12,987 households out of a total sample of 56,734 households.

Because the LTC is a sample of persons and the AHS is a sample of households, the next step was to identify households with more than one elderly member. To include these cases without jeopardizing the integrity of the subsample, we rewrote each of these records as a separate case for each elderly individual in the household. All household information pertaining to each elderly individual was copied onto that individual's record. Each record was also assigned the full household weight. This process produced a subsample with 16,979 persons.

Third, because the LTC sample is restricted to frail elderly, we conducted a series of analyses to identify a small set of variables in the AHS that could be used to define frailty and to screen for cases that approximately matched the LTC sample. To qualify for inclusion in the LTC, an individual had to report the presence of at least one of nine needs on an expanded activity of daily living (ADL) scale or one of seven instrumental activities of daily living (IADL) needs; in each case, the need had to have existed for at least three months or was expected to persist for that long. Approximately 19 percent of the cases screened for the LTC met this definition of frailty. The AHS contains information on four of the nine ADLs (i.e., problems getting around inside, getting around outside, toileting, and bedridden) but none of the IADLs; nor does the AHS contain information about duration of a problem. Preliminary analysis within the LTC revealed a very high correlation between the four items included in the AHS and several of the remaining ADL items only in the LTC (e.g., 83 percent of those with toileting problems also have bathing problems). High correlations were also observed between the ADL items in the AHS and several of the IADL items (e.g., 97 percent of those with toileting problems and 95 percent of those reporting problems getting around inside also have problems shopping for groceries). Thus it was decided that any person 65 or older in the AHS who reported at least one of these ADL items should be included in the subsample. The AHS also included a fifth ADL-like measure--problems negotiating stairs--which we decided to include as well: only 76 individuals in the AHS are included in the match sample on the basis of this single measure only.

Clearly, this screen alone would be more restrictive than the LTC screen because it includes people with one of five possible problems as opposed to persons with one of 16. Therefore a second set of variables, health/physical conditions, was examined in an effort to broaden the screen. These variables are also highly correlated with the LTC screening measures. Twenty of the 33 conditions asked about in the LTC are also included in the AHS. Without the guidance of any substantive work on the relationship between specific health conditions and the presence of persistent ADL or IADL needs, we adopted a practical criterion. We tested several thresholds or standards to find the one that best met two conditions: the distribution of the resulting subsample across demographic characteristics sufficiently approximated the distributions for the LTC sample, and the fraction of cases "screened in" approximated the fraction screened into the LTC (about 19 percent). The thresholds tested and the fraction of the sample encompassed by each are as follows:

Presence of any of the five ADLs or	Unweighted Number of Persons	Unweighted Percentage
1. at least one health condition	= 6,939	40.9
2. at least two health conditions	= 2,538	14.9
3. at least three health conditions	= 1,578	9.3
4. at least four health conditions	= 1,407	8.3

Version 2 screens in about 15 percent of the cases, which most closely approximates the target of 19 percent. The sample represented by version 2 was examined further through cross-tabular analysis to see whether the distribution of sex, age, and household size for the resulting subsample was consistent between the two data bases. In most cases, the resulting distributions were quite consistent. (Distributions are available from the authors.) On these two bases, then, version 2 was chosen as the criterion for selecting the AHS subsample. This sample contains 2,538 people: 1,266 with at least one ADL and 1,442 with at least two of 20 medical conditions. The final step in preparing the AHS subsample extract was to exclude owners because the present research focuses on elderly renters. [1]

IMPUTATION OF AHS VALUES TO THE LTC

The preparation of the AHS subsample resulted in a data base of frail elderly appropriate for statistical matching. This subsample consisted of 732 renters 65 or older with at least one of five ADL impairments or at least two of 20 health conditions included in both the AHS and LTC.

The AHS subsample was used as the source of information on whether the elderly renter lived in assisted housing. This indicator was appended to the LTC by predicting its value in the matched AHS subsample and then imputing this predicted value to the LTC. The key components of the imputation are as follows:

1.   Using the AHS subsample, we specified a regression equation in which the dependent variable was whether the elderly renter lived in assisted housing and the independent variables were restricted to those present in both the AHS and the LTC. Specifically, the probability of living in assisted housing was estimated as a function of age, sex, race, income, education, geographic region, metropolitan status, type of structure, and the presence or absence of dwelling unit modifications.

2.   Because the dependent variable is dichotomous (1 = lives in assisted housing; 0 = otherwise), a logistic regression procedure was used to make the prediction.[2] The specifications of the model are shown in table A.1. The logit transformation produces the following equation in which P is the probability that the dependent variable equals one:

$$P = 1/(1 + e^{**(-(a+bX))})$$

3.   The values of the constant term and coefficients from the right-hand side of the solved predictive equation in the AHS were then assigned to the LTC data set. This procedure resulted in a probability that each sample person in the LTC lived in assisted

housing. The value of this probability ranged between 0 and 1.

4.   Because the dependent variable is dichotomous but the predictive equation results in a distribution of values between 0 and 1, it was necessary to set a critical value or "cut off" for assigning some cases to the "1" category (i.e., living in assisted housing) and some to the "0" category (i.e., not living in assisted housing). In setting this critical value, we should achieve two preliminary objectives: first, that individuals are not misclassified as living in assisted housing when they do not (Type I error) or as not living in assisted housing when they do (Type II error) and second, that the resulting prevalence rate of residence in assisted housing resemble the "true" rate (as measured in the "parent" data set, the AHS). The threshold for this classification is somewhat arbitrary. The most obvious place to start is a cutoff value of .5: that is, any case with a predicted probability of over 50 percent was classified as living in assisted housing; those with a probability below 50 percent were classified as not living in assisted housing. We also tested two other thresholds: .33 and .67.

5.   In order to evaluate the relative merits of these three critical values, we compared the predicted assignment of cases to residence in, or out of, assisted housing using each of the three critical values to the actual distribution of cases in the AHS, the parent data file. As shown in table A.2, the .5 threshold produced the fewest misclassifications, the .67 threshold produced the fewest Type I errors, and the .33 threshold produced the predicted total number of cases living in assisted housing that is closest to the actual number in that status. The .5 level, therefore, produced the best overall categorization of cases.

6.   In addition to the relative merits of the .5 level in the assignment of cases, it also resulted in an estimated 20.4 percent of the frail elderly in the LTC living in assisted housing. This rate compares quite favorably with the 19.9 percent produced by the AHS.

Therefore, the .5 threshold was chosen for the assignment of cases in the LTC on the assisted housing variable.

7.   An additional insight provided by the comparison of the three alternative critical values is that the estimates produced by the predictive equation were quite robust. As shown in tables A.3 and A.4, two groups of characteristics of frail elderly living in assisted housing are quite stable across these three critical values: institutional risk and functional impairments and demographic, locational, and economic attributes.

8.   The pattern of missing data in the imputed assisted housing variable was checked to determine whether statistical weights were needed to adjust for the nonrandom distribution of missing values. Missing values occur in the LTC when any of the independent variables from the regression equation are missing. Fortunately, as shown in table A.5, the distribution of missing data was quite similar among population subgroups (e.g., race, whether individual lives alone, presence of ADL limitations). Therefore, there was no need to develop a missing data weighting scheme.

9.   Finally, cross-tabulations were prepared that distributed the imputed variable across several demographic and locations measures for both the LTC (the recipient data set) and the AHS (the donor data set). A subset of these joint distributions are shown in table A.6. These cross-tabs reveal good consistency across the two data bases.[3]

Notes, appendix A

1. No cash renters were included in the subsample.

2. It has been clearly documented that when ordinary least squares (OLS) is applied to a binary dependent variable, the error term is heteroscedastic and predicted values may lie outside the 0-1 range. An OLS regression was also used, and indeed, the logit transformation produced more robust predictions.

3.   It should also be noted that since there is a four-year time difference between the 1978 AHS and the LTC, gross rent was inflated from 1978 to 1982.

TABLE A.1   LOGISTIC REGRESSION PROCEDURE

Dependent Variable: XGOVA[a]

722 Observations
578 XGOVA = 0
144 XGOVA = 1
10 Observations deleted because of missing values

Variable	Mean	Minimum	Maximum	Range
XZINC78	5934.9	1500	55000	53500
XWRACE	0.861496	0	1	1
XHSGRAD	0.279778	0	1	1
XNCENTRL	0.256233	0	1	1
XSOUTH	0.331025	0	1	1
XWEST	0.138504	0	1	1
XINSMSA	0.616343	0	1	1
XTYPEAPT	0.484765	0	1	1
XTYPESFD	0.493075	0	1	1
XHUMOD	0.16482	0	1	1
XHAGE	75.3366	65	97	32
XSEX	0.693906	0	1	1

-2 log likelihood for model containing intercept only = 721.47

Model chi-square = 160.51 with 12 D.F.   (Score Stat. P = 0.0)
Convergence obtained in 7 iterations.   R=0.473
Max absolute derivative = 0.2367D-06.   -2 LOG L = 535.76
Model chi-square = 185.71 with 12 D.F.   (-2 LOG L.R.) P = 0.0

Variable	Beta	Standard error	Chi-square	P	R
INTERCEPT	1.39341909	1.69404259	0.68	0.4108	
XZINC78	-0.00021218	0.00003901	29.58	0.0000	-0.196
XWRACE	-1.26096598	0.32186640	15.35	0.0001	-0.136
XHSGRAD	-0.12246245	0.26040208	0.22	0.6382	0.000
XNCENTRL	0.42307292	0.29910855	2.00	0.1572	0.001
XSOUTH	-0.25292907	0.31868649	0.63	0.4274	0.000
XWEST	-0.03962711	0.35202348	0.01	0.9104	0.000
XINSMSA	0.28856295	0.27416635	1.11	0.2926	0.000
XTYPEAPT	2.10493006	1.09631399	3.69	0.0549	0.048
XTYPESFD	0.06507073	1.09933072	0.00	0.9528	0.000
XHUMOD	1.55092496	0.26281458	34.82	0.0000	0.213
XHAGE	-0.03511580	0.01689140	4.32	0.0376	-0.057
XSEX	0.12525973	0.25677289	0.24	0.6257	0.000

Fraction of concordant pairs of predicted probabilities & responses rank   0.828
Correlation between predicted probability and response   0.668

Notes:

a. Variable definitions are as follows:

XZINC78	1978 total household income
XWRACE	If household head is white = 1; else = 0
XHSGRAD	If household head is high school graduate = 1
XNCENTRL	If household lives in north central region = 1; else = 0
XSOUTH	If household lives in south = 1; else = 0
XWEST	If household lives in west = 1; else = 0
XINSMSA	If household lives in an SMSA = 1; else = 0
XTYPEAPT	If household lives in a 3 or more unit apartment building = 1; else = 0
XTYPESFD	If household lives in a single family detached house, rowhouse, or duplex = 1; else = 0
XHUMOD	If housing unit contains any of the following features: extra handrails or grabbars, ramps, elevator, extra wide doors or hallways, raised toilet or bathroom designed for wheelchair = 1; else = 0.
XHAGE	Age of head, in years
XSEX	If household head is male = 1; female = 0

TABLE A.2   PREDICTED VERSUS ACTUAL ASSIGNMENT
OF CASES TO RESIDENCE IN, OR OUT OF,
GOVERNMENT-ASSISTED HOUSING USING
DIFFERENT THRESHOLDS IN THE AHS
SUBSAMPLE

	Threshold = .50 Actual	
Predicted	No	Yes
No	555	89
Yes	23	55

	Threshold = .67 Actual	
Predicted:	No	Yes
No	571	114
Yes	7	30

	Threshold = .33 Actual:	
Predicted	No	Yes
No	512	63
Yes	66	81

TABLE A.3 PERCENTAGE OF THE FRAIL ELDERLY IN
GOVERNMENT-ASSISTED HOUSING AT RISK OR
WITH FUNCTIONAL IMPAIRMENTS, BY VARIOUS
PREDICTION THRESHOLDS

	Prediction Threshold		
Institutional risk	33%	50%	68%
Institutionalized within 2 years or on nursing home waiting list	20.3	17.7	18.8
Institutionalized within 2 years for 90 days or more	8.6	7.5	10.3
Functional limitations			
Needs assistance with at least 1 ADL[a]	31.3	28.4	27.2
Needs assistance with either eating or toileting	8.2	6.9	6.9
Needs assistance with at least 1 IADL[b]	98.5	96.8	95.0
Cognitive impairment[c]			
Yes	28.0	28.0	31.2

Source: Linked 1978 AHS and 1982-84 National Long-Term
Care Surveys.

Note: Unweighted case counts for column 1 = 387, column 2 =
268, column 3 = 124.

a.   ADLS are activities of dailing living that include: transfer,
mobility, dressing, bathing, toileting, and eating.
b.   IADLs are instrumental activities of dailing living that
include heavy housework, light housework, laundry, preparing
meals, shopping for groceries, getting around outside, going
places beyond walking distance managing money, and making
telephone calls.
c.   Sample individuals were considered to have cognitive
impairments if they scored below average (for the LTC sample
as a whole) on a standardized test of cognitive impairment, the
Short Portable Mental Status Quiz.

TABLE A.4   DISTRIBUTION OF CHARACTERISTICS FOR THE
FRAIL ELDERLY IN GOVERNMENT-ASSISTED
HOUSING, BY VARIOUS PREDICTION
THRESHOLDS

| | Prediction Threshold | | |
	33%	50%	67%
Sex			
Male	18.0	16.1	14.2
Female	82.0	83.9	85.8
Age			
65-69	26.1	27.0	33.7
70-74	24.8	28.6	30.9
75-79	18.1	18.0	17.4
80-84	16.2	14.9	10.5
85-89	11.1	10.2	6.1
90 or more	3.8	1.4	1.4
MEAN (years)	75.6	74.8	73.5
Race			
White	73.7	68.1	60.2
Other	26.3	31.9	39.8
Education			
High school graduate	30.0	30.7	26.3
Support			
Informal	75.5	75.0	77.1
Formal	39.8	40.1	38.2
Income			
$0-4,999	76.8	82.1	90.1
5,000-6,999	16.4	16.8	9.3
7,000-8,999	5.3	6.8	0.0
9,000-9,999	0.4	0.3	0.7
10,000 or more	1.1	0.0	0.0
MEAN	$3,865.00	$3,547.00	$2,970.00

TABLE A.4 (Continued)

| | Prediction Threshold | | |
	33%	50%	67%
Gross Rent			
$ < 100	46.7	51.6	59.5
100-149	22.0	24.7	22.3
150-199	10.8	8.7	8.9
200-249	8.5	6.3	4.0
250-299	6.4	4.5	4.0
300-349	2.5	1.5	0.0
350-399	1.9	1.0	0.7
400 or more	3.0	1.7	0.6
Mean	$194.3	$191.1	$180.0
Number of stories			
4 stories or more	24.2	26.3	21.4
Region			
Northeast	34.8	35.9	60.5
Northwest	18.3	18.8	6.7
South	15.9	13.5	8.7
West	30.9	31.9	24.2
Metropolitan status			
In SMSA	69.7	71.5	72.9

Source: Linked 1978 AHS and 1982-84 National Long-Term Care Surveys.

Note: Unweighted case counts for column 1 = 387, column 2 = 268, and column 3 = 124.

TABLE A.5   PERCENTAGE AND NUMBER OF MISSING DATA CASES ON IMPUTED HOUSING ASSISTANCE VARIABLE, BY DEMOGRAPHIC AND OTHER CHARACTERISTICS

Sex

Male	Female
15.5% (68/438)	20.8% (242/1161)

Age

65-69	70-74	75-79	80-84	85-89	90+
12.3% (35/284)	16.2% (55/340)	21.9% (78/357)	19.8% (62/313)	27.0% (58/215)	24.4% (22/90)

Metro Status

In SMSA	Not in SMSA
21.3% (184/862)	16.9% (124/735)

Number of Stories

<4	4 or more
1.9% (21/1109)	1.5% (3/203)

Region

No. Central	South	West	No.East
20.5% (74/361)	15.2% (77/508)	16.9% (45/266)	24.6% (114/464)

Race

White	Nonwhite
18.1% (241/331)	16.7% (40/239)

Income

<$5,000	$5,000-7,000	$7,000-9,000	$9,000-10,000	$10,000+
3.7% (30/805)	3.1% (7/228)	2.3% (3/133)	3.5% (1/29)	6.3% (9/144)

Lives Alone

Yes	No
18.5% (152/824)	20.4% (158/775)

Spouse in Household

Yes	No
14.4% (62/431)	21.2% (248/1168)

Institutionalized w/in 2 yrs.

Yes	No
22.7% (68/300)	18.6% (242/1299)

Type of Structure

Detached	Multi-unit	Mobile Home
19.7% (126/641)	18.5% (163/879)	14.6% (6/41)

Whether High School Graduate

Yes	No
18.4% (86/467)	16.2% (175/1083)

ADL Limited[a]

Yes	No
19.4% (254/1313)	19.6% (56/286)

IADL Limited[b]

Yes	No
19.6% (250/1276)	18.6% (60/323)

Institutionalized for 90+ days w/in 2 yrs.

Yes	No
24.2% (40/165)	18.8% (270/1434)

Source: Linked 1978 AHS and 1982-84 National Long-Term Care Survey.

Note: The top number is the percent of all imputed cases that is missing for the particular category; in parentheses, the numerator is the unweighted number of missing observations and the denominator is the total imputed observations.

a.   ADLs are activities of daily living that include: transfer, mobility, dressing, bathing, toileting, and eating.

b.   IADLs are instrumental activities of daily living that include: heavy housework, light housework, laundry, preparing meals, shopping for groceries, getting around outside, going places beyond walking distance, managing money, and making telephone calls.

TABLE A.6 CHARACTERISTICS OF FRAIL PERSONS 65 AND
OLDER BY IMPUTED VARIABLE: "LIVING IN
ASSISTED HOUSING" FOR DONOR DATA SET
(AHS) AND RECIPIENT DATA SET (LTC)

	AHS	LTC
Sex		
Male	24.0	16.0
Female	76.0	84.0
Age		
65-69	21.5	27.0
70-74	31.6	28.6
75-79	21.7	18.0
80-84	16.7	14.9
85-89	4.2	10.2
90 or older	4.1	1.4
Race		
White	79.7	68.1
Nonwhite	20.3	31.9
Household composition		
Male living alone	15.4	8.8
Female living alone	63.6	65.3
Couple	15.6	17.5
Living with others	5.3	8.5
Income		
$ < 5,000	79.9	72.1
5,000-6,999	9.0	16.8
7,000-8,999	7.7	0.8
9,000-9,999	1.1	0.3
10,000 or more	2.4	0
Metropolitan status		
In SMSA	80.7	71.5
Outside SMSA	19.2	28.5

TABLE A.6 (continued)

	AHS	LTC
Number of stories		
< 4	63.9	73.7
4 or More	36.1	26.3
Rent		
$ < 100	73.3	51.6
100-149	12.3	24.7
150-199	8.0	8.3
200-249	4.4	6.3
250-299	1.6	4.5
300-349	0	1.5
350-399	0.3	1.0
400 or more	0	1.7
Region		
Northeast	33.2	31.9
North Central	30.4	35.9
South	20.6	18.8
West	15.9	13.5

Source: Column 1 from 1978 AHS; column 2 from linked 1978 AHS and 1982-84 National Long-Term Care Surveys.

Note: Unweighted case counts for column 1 = 144 and column 2 = 268.

a. In the AHS column, living alone was defined as living in a household with no other adults.

Appendix B
SOURCES OF ERROR IN ESTIMATES AND A METHOD FOR
DEVELOPING CONFIDENCE INTERVALS

A primary goal of this research is to estimate the proportion of
the frail elderly living in government-assisted housing who have
particular functional impairments or are at risk of
institutionalization. The 1982-84 National Long-Term Care
Survey (LTC) is the source of data on the proportion of frail
elderly renter with functional impairments or at institutional
risk. Through the statistical imputation approach described in
appendix A, the 1978 American Housing Survey (AHS) is used
to identify LTC survey respondents who are most likely to be
living in government-assisted housing. This procedure carries
imprecision at three steps:

1.   Using different definitions of frailty in AHS and
LTC. The first source of error is in the two definitions
used (or criteria applied) to assign membership to the
frail elderly subgroup. In short, in detailing the
assumptions on which the final estimate is based, we
maintained the assumption that the frail group
identified in the AHS corresponds closely to the LTC
frail elderly group of renters. This close categorization
may be based on either the fact that the definitions of
"frail" in each data set produce similar categorizations
of the resulting subsample along demographic or
economic characteristics or that the two subsamples
are similar with respect to residence in government
assisted housing, functional impairment, and risk of
institutionalization.
        Because the AHS did not include screening
measures identical to those used to select the LTC
sample of frail elderly, a substitute assignment rule
was developed. Appendix A discusses the
compatibility of the two screening approaches, which
increases confidence that the two screening methods

would produce similar allocations into the frail and nonfrail groups. But it is impossible to determine the type of error introduced when using different criteria for defining frailty.

2.   <u>Basing residence in government-assisted housing on a regression equation.</u> The second source of error is the use of a regression equation estimated with the AHS data to predict whether individuals in the LTC survey live in government housing. When regression equations are used for prediction, there are two sources of error: one emanating from the disturbance term in the regression equation (unavoidable randomness) and the other from using estimates of the true coefficients. Here we can get an idea of the effect of randomness by comparing the regression-predicted "probabilities" of being in government-assisted housing to whether the individuals actually lived in government housing. As discussed in appendix A, the logit prediction model produced relatively robust estimates, reasonably good alignment between predicted and actual place of residence (i.e., in or out of government assisted housing), and a similar prevalence rate of residence in assisted housing. However, imprecision still remains in the allocation of cases in the LTC to assisted or unassisted housing.

3.   <u>Relying on surveys with complex sampling designs.</u> All the estimated proportions presented in this report are based on a sample rather than on total population. Therefore these estimates are subject to the usual <u>variance</u> that is associated with any estimated proportion and to a <u>design effect</u> associated with the fact that the AHS and LTC were based on a multistage design and not on simple random samples.

As noted, there is no way to quantify the errors that are associated with steps 1 and 2. However, we calculated standard errors and confidence intervals for key estimates to account for variances and design effects. Two features of these calculations should be noted:

✦ The standard errors do <u>not</u> reflect the fact that the frail elderly have been classified as residing in government-assisted housing on the basis of an estimated logit model. As noted, this model-based prediction is an additional source of error that cannot be quantified readily. Therefore the true standard errors and confidence intervals are likely to be higher and larger than those estimated in chapter 2.

✦ A design effect of 1.50 has been assumed due to the multistage cluster sample design of both the AHS and the LTC. It is likely that the design effect is actually lower, a fact that would mean that the standard errors and confidence intervals provided in chapter 2 are actually lower and smaller.

Appendix C
SUPPLEMENTARY TABULATIONS

TABLE C.1   CHARACTERISTICS OF THE ELDERLY LIVING
IN GOVERNMENT-ASSISTED HOUSING
(Weighted Percentages)

	Frail Elderly	All Elderly
Sex		
Male	24.0	28.2
Female	76.0	71.8
Age		
65-69	21.5	27.3
70-74	31.6	29.5
75-79	21.7	21.3
80-84	16.7	13.4
85-89	4.2	6.4
90 or older	4.1	2.1
Race		
White	79.7	77.2
Nonwhite	20.3	22.8
Household composition[a]		
Male living alone	15.4	13.7
Female living alone	63.6	54.8
Couple	15.6	22.6
Living with others	5.3	8.8
Income		
$ < 5000	79.9	74.3
5000-6999	9.0	14.4
7000-8999	7.7	5.1
9000-9999	1.1	1.9
10,000 or more	2.4	4.4

Table C.1 (continued)

	Frail Elderly	All Elderly
Metropolitan status		
In SMSA	80.7	75.2
Outside SMSA	19.2	24.8
Number of stories:		
< 4	63.9	65.0
4 or more	36.1	35.0
Gross rent		
$ < 100	73.3	65.8
100-149	12.3	16.7
150-199	8.0	9.3
200-249	4.4	5.5
250-299	1.6	1.6
300-349	0	0.2
350-399	0.3	0.8
400 or more	0	0.2
Region		
Northeast	33.2	32.2
North Central	30.4	28.5
South	20.6	22.4
West	15.9	16.8

Source: 1978 National American Housing Survey.

Note: Unweighted case counts for column 1 = 144 and column 2 = 599.

a. For those living in assisted housing, living alone was defined as living in a household with no other adults.

TABLE C.2   CHARACTERISTICS OF ELDERLY RISK GROUPS
LIVING IN GOVERNMENT-ASSISTED HOUSING
Institutionalized within 2 Years for 90 Days or More
(Weighted Percentages)

	Frail Elderly	All Elderly
Sex		
Male	0[a]	0[a]
Female	8.9	2.5
Age		
65-69	3.2	0.8
70-74	3.9	0.9
75-79	7.2	1.4
80-84	19.8	5.3
85-89	9.3	3.5
90 or older	22.3	3.6
Race		
White	9.2	1.9
Nonwhite	3.9	1.1
Household composition		
Male living alone	0	0
Female living alone	9.7	2.8
Couple	4.9	0.9
Living with others	3.2	0.7
Income		
$ < 5000	8.1	2.1
5000-6999	4.9	1.4
7000-8999	0	0
9000-9999	0	0
10,000 or more	0	0
Metropolitan status		
In SMSA	9.1	2.1
Outside SMSA	3.3	0.9

	Frail Elderly	All Elderly
Number of stories		
< 4	8.3	2.2
4 or more	5.1	0.9
Gross rent		
$ < 100	9.2	1.7
100-149	5.0	1.8
150-199	0	0
200-249	18.7	5.1
250-299	0	0
300-349	0	NA
350-399	35.1	10.7
400 or more	0	NA
Region		
Northeast	5.2	1.2
North Central	9.5	2.8
South	8.5	1.7
West	6.0	1.1

Source: Linked 1978 AHS and 1982-84 National Long-Term Care Surveys.

Notes:
1. Unweighted case count for column 1 = 268; case count for column 2 derived from AHS. (See table 2.4, Note.)
2. NA = not available.
3. For those living in assisted housing, living alone was defined as living in a household with no other adults.
[a] The interpretation of the first estimate on the table is as follows: of the frail elderly who live in assisted housing, 0 percent of the males are at risk of permanent institutionalization.

TABLE C.3   CHARACTERISTICS OF ELDERLY RISK GROUPS
LIVING IN GOVERNMENT-ASSISTED HOUSING:
Institutionalized within 2 Years or on a Nursing
Home Waiting List (Weighted Percentages)

	Frail Elderly	All Elderly
Sex		
Male	13.5	1.8
Female	18.5	5.2
Age		
65-69	5.9	1.4
70-74	13.8	3.2
75-79	17.1	3.4
80-84	30.8	8.1
85-89	36.8	14.1
90 or older	54.3	8.9
Race		
White	22.7	4.8
Nonwhite	7.1	2.4
Household Composition		
Male living alone	12.3	1.9
Female living alone	19.9	5.6
Couple	16.7	3.1
Living with others	8.5	1.9
Income		
$ < 5000	18.8	5.0
5000-6999	13.4	3.7
7000-8999	0	0
9000-9999	0	0
10,000 or more	0	0

TABLE C.3 (continued)

	Frail Elderly	All Elderly
Metropolitan status:		
In SMSA	17.0	3.8
Outside SMSA	19.6	5.4
Number of stories		
< 4	20.8	5.6
4 or more	9.2	1.6
Gross rent		
$ < 100	20.8	3.9
100-149	12.0	4.2
150-199	8.3	1.9
200-249	18.7	5.1
250-299	31.3	21.0
300-349	0	NA
350-399	35.1	10.7
400 or more	20.4	NA
Region		
Northeast	9.6	2.3
North Central	27.4	8.2
South	13.2	2.6
West	17.3	3.3

Source: Linked 1978 AHS and 1982-84 National Long-Term Care Surveys.
Notes:
1. Unweighted case count for column 1 = 268. Case count for column 2 derived from AHS. (See table 2.4, note 2.)
2. For interpretation of estimates, see table C.2, footnote a.
3. NA = not available.
4. For those living in assisted housing, living alone was defined as living in a household with no other adults.

TABLE C.4   CHARACTERISTICS OF ELDERLY RISK GROUPS
LIVING IN GOVERNMENT-ASSISTED HOUSING:
Needs Assistance with at Least One ADL
(Weighted Percentages)

	Frail Elderly	All Elderly
Sex		
Male	39.3	5.3
Female	26.3	7.3
Age		
65-69	23.7	5.6
70-74	34.3	7.9
75-79	22.3	4.5
80-84	31.4	8.3
85-89	31.0	11.8
90 or older	21.8	3.6
Race		
White	25.7	5.4
Nonwhite	34.0	11.3
Household Composition		
Male living alone	21.7	3.3
Female living alone	18.4	5.2
Couple	53.2	9.8
Living with others	60.2	13.8
Income		
$ < 5000	28.0	7.4
5000-6999	27.5	7.6
7000-8999	50.1	1.9
9000-9999	100.0	3.9
10,000 or more	0	0

Table C.4 (continued)

	Frail Elderly	All Elderly
Metropolitan status		
In SMSA	28.2	6.4
Outside SMSA	28.7	7.9
Numbers of stories		
< 4	28.6	7.7
4 or more	27.6	4.9
Gross rent		
$ < 100	21.8	4.1
100-149	30.1	10.6
150-199	37.0	8.3
200-249	35.4	9.6
250-299	41.6	27.8
300-349	24.0	NA
350-399	100.0	30.6
400 or more	57.2	NA
Region		
Northeast	25.1	5.9
North Central	29.0	8.7
South	36.5	7.3
West	23.0	4.4

Source: Linked 1978 AHS and 1982-84 National Long-Term Care Surveys.
Notes:
1. ADLs are activities of daily living that include: transfer, mobility, dressing, bathing, toileting, or eating.
2. Unweighted case count for column 1 = 268; case count for column 2 derived from AHS. (See table 2.4, note 2.)
3. For interpretation of estimates, see table C.2, note a.
4. NA = not available.
5. For those living in assisted housing, living alone was defined as living in a household with no other adults.

TABLE C.5   CHARACTERISTICS OF ELDERLY RISK GROUPS
LIVING IN GOVERNMENT-ASSISTED HOUSING:
Needs Assistance with Either Eating or Toileting
(Weighted Percentages)

	Frail Elderly	All Elderly
Sex		
Male	9.0	1.2
Female	6.5	1.8
Age		
64-69	5.7	1.3
70-74	7.5	1.7
75-79	5.7	1.1
80-84	7.4	2.0
85-89	7.4	2.8
90 or older	21.8	3.6
Race		
White	6.4	1.3
Nonwhite	7.8	2.6
Household Composition		
Male living alone	8.5	1.3
Female living alone	2.2	0.6
Couple	13.0	2.1
Living with others	28.5	6.5
Income		
$ < 5000	6.8	1.8
5000 - 6999	3.6	1.0
7000 - 8999	50.1	5.1
9000 - 9999	100.0	3.9
10,000 or more	0	0

Table C.5 (continued)

	Frail Elderly	All Elderly
Region		
Northeast	8.0	1.9
North Central	5.0	1.5
South	9.9	2.0
West	5.2	1.0
Metropolitan status		
In SMSA	5.7	1.3
Outside SMSA	9.8	2.7
Number of stories		
< 4	7.5	3.0
4 or more	10.4	2.4
Gross rent		
$ < 100	4.0	0.8
100-149	8.3	2.9
150-199	11.7	2.6
200-249	0	0
250-299	7.8	5.2
300-349	24.0	NA
350-399	31.2	9.5
400 or more	39.4	NA
Mean	185.0	0
Median	176.0	0

Source: Linked 1978 AHS and 1982-84 National Long-Term Care Surveys.
Notes:
1. Unweighted case count for column 1 = 268; case count for column 2 derived from AHS. (See table 2.4, Note.)
2. For interpretation of estimates, see table C.2, note a.
3. For those living in assisted housing, living alone was defined as living in a household with no other adults.

TABLE C.6   CHARACTERISTICS OF ELDERLY RISK GROUPS
              LIVING IN GOVERNMENT-ASSISTED HOUSING:
              Needs Assistance with at Least One IADL
              (Weighted Percentages)

	Frail Elderly	All Elderly
Sex		
Male	95.7	13.0
Female	97.1	27.0
Age		
65-69	94.4	22.2
70-74	96.0	22.1
75-79	97.1	19.5
80-84	100.0	26.5
85-89	100.0	38.2
90 or older	100.0	16.3
Race		
White	97.8	20.6
Nonwhite	94.8	31.6
Household Composition		
Male living alone	92.0	14.0
Female living alone	97.0	27.5
Couple	100.0	18.4
Living with others	93.9	21.5
Income		
$ < 5000	96.2	25.3
5000-6999	100.0	27.7
7000-8999	100.0	3.7
9000-9999	100.0	3.9
10,000 or more	0	0
Metropolitan status		
In SMSA	96.0	21.8
Outside SMSA	98.9	27.1

Table C.6 (continued)

	Frail Elderly	All Elderly
Number of stories		
< 4	97.2	26.2
4 or more	95.9	17.2
Rent		
$100	95.5	17.9
100-149	96.5	33.9
150-199	100.0	22.5
200-249	100.0	27.2
250-299	100.0	66.9
300-349	100.0	NA
350-399	100.0	30.6
400 or more	100.0	NA
Region		
Northeast	96.6	22.8
North Central	96.5	29.0
South	95.6	19.0
West	100.0	19.1

Source: Linked 1978 AHS and 1982-84 National Long-Term Care Surveys.
Notes:
1. ADLs are activities of daily living that include: transfer, mobility, dressing, bathing, toileting, and eating.

2. Unweighted case count for column 1 = 268; case count for column 2 derived from AHS. (See table 2.4, note.)

3. For interpretation of estimates, see table C.2, note a.

4. NA = not available.

TABLE C.7   CHARACTERISTICS OF ELDERLY RISK GROUPS
LIVING IN GOVERNMENT-ASSISTED HOUSING:
Has Cognitive Impairment[a] (Weighted Percentages)

	Frail Elderly	All Elderly
Sex		
Male	17.5	2.3
Female	30.0	8.3
Age		
65-69	24.9	5.9
70-74	26.9	6.2
75-79	25.5	5.1
80-84	32.4	8.6
85-89	40.9	15.6
90 or older	0	0
Race		
White	22.1	4.6
Nonwhite	40.6	13.6
Household Composition		
Male living alone	28.1	4.3
Female living alone	28.3	8.0
Couple	19.8	3.7
Living with others	42.5	9.7
Income		
$ < 5000	30.6	8.1
5000-6999	12.8	3.5
7000-8999	50.1	1.9
9000-9999	100.0	3.9
10,000 or more	0	0

Table C.7 (continued)

	Frail Elderly	All Elderly
Metropolitan status		
In SMSA	29.3	6.6
Outside SMSA	24.6	6.7
Number of stories		
< 4	27.3	7.4
4 or More	29.8	11.2
Rent		
$ < 100	29.2	5.5
100-149 32.8	11.5	
150-199	15.7	3.5
200-249	31.5	8.5
250-299	16.8	11.2
300-349	0	NA
350-399	33.8	10.3
400 or More	23.0	NA
Region		
Northeast	25.6	6.0
North Central	24.0	7.2
South	36.7	7.3
West	32.0	6.1

Source: Linked 1978 AHS and 1982-84 National Long-Term Care Surveys.
Notes:
1. Sample individuals were considered to have cognitive impairments if they scored below average (for the LTC sample as a whole) on a standardized test of cognitive impairment, the Short Portable Mental Status Quiz.
2. Unweighted case count for column 1 = 268; case count for column 2 derived from AHS. (See table 2.4, note 2.)
3. For interpretation of estimates, see table C.2, note a.
4. NA = not available.
5. For those living in assisted housing, living alone was defined as living in a household with no other adults.

TABLE C.8   COMPARATIVE AGE DISTRIBUTIONS OF ELDERLY
HOUSEHOLDS IN GOVERNMENT-ASSISTED
HOUSING, 1978 AND 1983 (Weighted Percentages)

| | Lives in Government-Assisted Housing | |
	1978	1983
Age		
62-64	6.7-12.5	7.9-13.1
65-69	18.6-27.0	14.5-21.1
70-74	22.5-31.3	21.8-29.2
75-79	15.9-23.7	17.7-24.7
80-84	9.3-16.3	12.5-18.7
85-89	3.8-8.6	4.5- 8.7
90 or older	0.6-3.4	1.3-4.1

Source: 1978 and 1983 National American Housing Surveys.

Notes:

1. Unweighted case counts for column 1 = 583 and column 2 = 781.

2. The range represents the 95 percent confidence interval around the estimated proportion. (See Appendix B.)

3. Sample includes all households in which at least one person was 62 years of age or older.

Appendix   D
STATE PROGRAM DESCRIPTIONS

MARYLAND

Overview

Maryland's Sheltered Housing program was initiated in 1976 and is the oldest state-funded congregate program in the country. The program is a housing alternative for frail elderly that combines shelter with meals, housekeeping and personal services.

The sheltered housing program has two components: a multifamily program under which supportive services are provided to elders residing in their own apartments and a group home program, begun in 1986, under which residents receive supportive services in shared homes. Sheltered housing serves approximately 1,000 elders in 35 multifamily apartment buildings and 548 elders residing in 65 group homes. The average age of a Multifamily Sheltered Housing (MSH) participant is 81 years, and the average of the Group Home Sheltered Housing (GHSH) participant is 83 years.

Sponsors of congregate facilities are generally local public housing authorities or nonprofit organizations, which must be certified by the Maryland Office on Aging.

Housing Environment

The MSH program encompasses senior public and assisted housing as well as private apartment buildings. The majority of program participants reside in public or assisted housing. Congregate units are scattered throughout a building and are fully independent efficiency or one-bedroom units. Each building participating in the program has a congregate dining room.

To prevent an institutional atmosphere, no more than 20 percent of a building's total residents may participate in the

gram. However, the Office on Aging (OOA) reports that it
ill permit, on a case-by-case basis, individual projects to
exceed the 20 percent cap. A minimum of 10 residents in a
large multifamily apartment building is needed for the program
to be economically efficient.

GHSH operates in small housing facilities, where four to
15 elderly people share a single household. Typically,
individual residents have a private or semiprivate bedroom and
bathroom, but share the dining room, and other common
areas. Single-family homes, former convents, and converted
school buildings make up the group home facilities.

Target Population and Admission Criteria

Admission to sheltered housing is open to elderly persons who
are at least 62 years old and who need some assistance with
daily tasks but do not need constant medical or nursing care.

Maryland regulations state that applicants must be
"physically or mentally impaired," defined as a "condition which
inhibits a person's ability to perform one or more activities of
daily living (ADL)." State regulations also set an upper limit on
assistance needs by requiring an applicant to be "able to
function" in a congregate setting.

Each sheltered housing sponsor hires a site coordinator
whose duties include screening applicants for admission to the
program. The OOA has developed an assessment
questionnaire that must be completed by the site coordinator
during a personal interview with an applicant. It provides
detailed interview questions in six functional areas: physical
health, mental health, memory, physical maintenance, ADLS,
and instrumental activities of daily living (IADLs).

The coordinator rates applicants in each functional area
using a five-grade rating scale. The structure of the
questionnaire reinforces the general admission standard that
applicants in need of constant medical or nursing supervision
are to be excluded, are those not requiring assistance in any
ADL.

Notwithstanding the standard needs assessment format, a
coordinator must exercise considerable discretion in judging
whether an applicant is eligible and suitable for sheltered

housing. However, the questionnaire is useful not only in guiding the coordinator in reaching an admission decision but also in its resulting in a document with systematic information on an applicant's capabilities and needs that can be used by the OOA to review the coordinator's decision. Interview questions with such a detailed structure would seem to be most appropriate in a program such as Maryland's, in which the admission decision is made by a coordinator not professionally trained in social work.

Types of Services

The MSH regulations require that participants be provided with: three meals a day seven days, at least one hour of housekeeping per week, at least one hour of personal services per week, and laundry services. Optional services include shopping, group activities, and transportation. GHSH residents are provided with the same service package and the additional service of 24-hour supervision.

The functional assessment questionnaire determines the needed level for use of each service. Reevaluation of participant service packages are performed sporadically when a participant demonstrates an overt physical or behavior problem.

Service Provision

Each sheltered housing facility has a site coordinator who determines admission into the program, plans a service package for each participant, and oversees delivery of services to participants. In addition to the coordinator, most multifamily projects have at least one housekeeper and a personal care staff person. Meals are prepared on site or may be prepared by a contractor and brought to the site.

As in most other congregate programs, the coordinator is the key staff position in the sheltered housing program. The Maryland OOA does not require any academic or professional experience for this position. However, it does require prior approval to a sponsor's hiring a coordinator. In addition, the

OOA requires that coordinators complete a training session on the sheltered housing program and the needs of elders.

Costs and Funding

The average monthly cost of these housing services is $300 per participant. The OOA provides a sliding subsidy for low-income participants. The average subsidy is $125 per assisted participant. There is a $500 cap on the monthly subsidy for group home participants; however, this subsidy covers rent as well as services. To be eligible for a subsidy, a participant's income must not be higher than 60 percent of the state's median income.

Sheltered housing is funded through annual appropriations by the legislature. For FY 1989, the multifamily appropriation was $1.25 million and the group home appropriation was $620,000. At least one of the three daily meals uses Title III-C funding. In addition, many projects use Title V Senior Aides to assist the on-site staff.

Evaluation

According to OOA, sheltered housing can be easily replicated in other states. Participants receive only services that they require. However, no formal evaluation has been conducted to determine the effectiveness of service tailoring. The OOA is considering a reduction in the three-meal-a-day requirement, recognizing that many participants do not want or need that many. However, the congregate meal provides an important opportunity for participants to socialize and permits the coordinator to spot potential problems that could require a reassessment of a participant's service package.

Source

Interview with Grace Smearman, Director, Sheltered Housing, Maryland Office on Aging; phone interview with John Listner, Group Sheltered Housing, Maryland Office on Aging.

MASSACHUSETTS

Overview

The Massachusetts congregate public housing program was formally established in 1978 after two years as a demonstration project. The program provides coordinated shelter and supportive services to low-income frail elderly residing in senior public housing. The program's objective is to assist the elderly in maintaining an independent life style and thus delay unnecessary institutionalization. The term "frail" elderly includes not only those who have some level of functional impairment but also those who are socially isolated.

Overall implementation of the program has been achieved through a working agreement among three state agencies. A memorandum of understanding (MOU) has been negotiated between the state's Executive Office of Communities and Development (EOCD), the Executive Office of Elder Affairs (EOEA), and the Department of Public Welfare (DPW). The MOU spells out each agency's authority and responsibility for the program and pledges cooperation and coordination among the three agencies and agencies under their authority.

The EOCD, which funds and administers the state's public housing program, including congregate housing facilities, is the primary funding agency for the program. Local housing authorities apply for construction grants to build congregate housing facilities or to renovate units within conventional buildings. The EOCD provides technical assistance during the design stage, provides operating subsidies, and oversees the management of the projects. As of August 1988, 397 congregate housing units have been occupied, with an additional 222 units expected to be occupied by the end of the year, for a total of 619 units in 42 projects.

The EOEA, the state's principal agency for elder services, finances and coordinates home care services for a broad range of the elderly, including congregate housing residents. A principal understanding in the MOU is that congregate housing residents have priority status over other elderly people for home care services provided under the state-funded Home Care Program.

The DPW provides financial assistance for health services to Medicaid-eligible residents. Approximately 140 Medicaid-certified home health agencies provide nursing, therapeutic, and home health aide services for Medicaid-eligible residents. The DPW also provides supplemental security income (SSI) and distributes food stamps to income-eligible congregate residents.

The EOCD, EOEA, and DPW have jointly developed guidelines for the development and operation of state-funded congregate housing projects. Because all supportive services come from existing local service providers (e.g., home care corporations or home health agencies), the guidelines stress careful planning and coordination at the local level to ensure that supportive services are available to meet the needs of congregate housing residents. A local MOU must be negotiated between the local housing authority and appropriate local service agencies before the EOCD approves congregate construction funds.

The EOCD reports that the program is a housing option for frail elderly and is not suitable for people requiring constant supervision. Supportive services assist residents in managing the daily activities of independent living and are provided on an as-needed basis to avoid unnecessary dependence on supportive services.

Housing Environment

The state-funded congregate housing program is limited to the state's public housing for the elderly. A congregate unit is a multibedroom apartment or shared house where all residents have, at a minimum, their own private bedrooms. Congregate facilities range from large shared apartments or clusters of small shared apartments imbedded in a conventional public housing facility to shared houses. Congregate housing facilities include as few as four and as many as 50 residents.

Residential buildings generally require some adaptive building modifications to comply with the state's congregate guidelines. A congregate housing facility must include at least two of the following: shared accessible community space, shared kitchen, shared dining facilities, and shared bathing facilities. The physical design of a congregate project seeks to encourage a shared living atmosphere that encourages interactions among residents.

Decisions concerning the design of a congregate facility will be influenced by local factors such as the level of frailty of the elderly population, the geographic area (rural or urban), the building site (new construction or rehabilitation), and local zoning regulations. State guidelines require that the housing authority organize a citizen advisory committee (CAC) to assist in the planning and design of the housing project. The CAC should consist of service agencies that may offer services needed by the congregate housing residents, including representatives of the local area agencies on aging and/or home care corporation, the local home health agency or visiting nurse association, the local council on aging, the local mental health clinic, and other local agencies that offer services appropriate for congregate housing residents.

Once a design plan is approved by the EOCD, a public bid takes place for the construction contract. During the construction phase, EOCD architects conduct periodic inspections of the construction site. After the congregate project is completed, the EOCD oversees the management of the facility, reviews and approves annual operating budgets, and ensures compliance with EOCD regulations on the maintenance and operation of public housing.

Housing authorities maintain separate waiting lists for congregate public housing units. Average waiting periods for congregate unit vacancies can range up to 18 months for some facilities.

Target Population and Admission Criteria

Applicants for state-funded congregate housing must meet two sets of admissions standards. First, the applicant must be at least 62 years old and must be income-eligible for public housing.[1]

Second, applicants must be determined suitable for congregate housing based on their functional capacity, health, social needs, and the likelihood that they will remain in a congregate facility for at least one year. State guidelines require that eligible applicants must be capable of independent living but require some support services to maintain a quality independent life style. No applicant should be accepted who requires constant supervision or requires maximal assistance to carry out the activities of daily living.

Appropriate applicants do not fit any ADL or IADL limitation range. Instead, state guidelines emphasize that a congregate project should, consistent with the availability of local support services, include a mix of residents with varying physical, mental, and emotional needs, including:

+ the physically well who do not desire to live alone,
+ the physically well who need emotional support,
+ the physically capable who need some informal or formal assistance,
+ the physically unwell or handicapped in need of formal and informal support, and
+ those suffering some mental incapacity who can do things slowly.

The Massachusetts program is somewhat unique in that it explicitly encourages a mixing of participants with varying levels of impairment, including some with no functional impairment. Massachusetts believes that such a mix permits the sharing of a combination of many strengths and affords each participant the opportunity to benefit from the special informal support gained from a shared living environment. Mixing participants with varying degrees of impairment is an effective way to avoid an institutional atmosphere. Moreover, mutual support by participants could also reduce the level of assistance required from the program, thereby reducing program costs.

An important constraint in evaluating congregate housing applicants is the scope, range, and commitment of local service providers. Because all supportive services are provided by local service providers, the range of available services will vary among communities. This factor will necessarily influence the type of applicants that can be accepted and how long residents may remain in the program. State guidelines emphasis that prior to a resident's admission to a congregate project, the level and type of supportive services that will be required by the applicant over time should be weighed against the community's ability to meet these needs.

An applicant's suitability for congregate housing is determined by a multidisciplinary assessment team (MAT). A MAT is organized for each project to review applications in accordance with state guidelines and periodically to review the service plan and health status of each resident. A MAT includes representatives from the local housing authority and from health, social service, and mental health agencies.

The MAT team leader is the congregate housing coordinator, who is responsible for screening prospective applicants and making recommendations to the MAT on final admission decisions. Two personal interviews are conducted with an applicant using two EOEA-designed needs assessment tools.

One of the assessment tools, the Client Needs Assessment Procedure (CNAP), is completed jointly by the congregate housing coordinator and a professional case manager. The CNAP seeks to ascertain the applicant's physical health, mental condition, and need for ADL and IADL assistance. The second assessment tool is completed by the coordinator and seeks to review the applicant's current living environment (housing, access to social services, and informal support network) and to assess the applicant's suitability for shared living. Attitudes and behavior influencing suitability for shared living are important factors because all living arrangements in the Massachusetts program involve shared living quarters in which individual bedrooms represent the only private space.

One of the two personal interviews is conducted at the applicant's home. Coordinators report that at-home interviews often permit the interviewer to observe the applicant's ability to carry out some ADLs, the extent of any social isolation of the applicant, and the applicant's current living arrangements. Further, the applicant's physician may be asked to complete an EOEA medical assessment form to determine the physical health of an applicant.

Relying on these assessment tools and the recommendation from the project coordinator, the MAT makes the final admission decision. State guidelines encourage participation of current congregate residents in the admission

decision process. Congregate residents should meet
applicants, and any resident concerns should be taken into
account.

Supportive Services

The scope and type of supportive services vary across
congregate housing projects and are dependent on the
capability of existing local community social service and health
agencies that serve the elderly. Supportive services needed for
a congregate project are identified during the planning stages of
the project and are committed in the local MOU negotiated
between the local housing authority and local service agencies.

Supportive services may include, but are not limited to,
case management, meal, homemaker, chore, home health,
personal care, and transportation services. Services are
provided on an as-needed basis determined by the initial CNAP
assessment and periodic reevaluations of resident needs.
Meals can be prepared by the residents themselves or by
homemakers, or they can be provided through Meals on
Wheels, or at "nutrition sites."

State guidelines permit flexibility in providing supportive
services to congregate housing residents. Various services can
be formally provided by a local service agency and congregate
project staff or informally provided by family, friends,
volunteers, and other congregate residents.

Formal service providers include home care corporations,
local home health agencies or visiting nurse associations,
councils on aging, mental health clinics, and other community
service agencies.

The EOEA reports that congregate residents receive the
majority of formal supportive services from the state-funded
Home Care Program. Under this program, the EOEA contracts
with local home care corporations or area agencies on aging to
provide services to congregate residents. Under the state MOU,
congregate residents have priority over other elders in the
delivery of home care services. The Home Care Program
provides the following services:

+ case management,
+ homemaker/personal care,
+ chore service,
+ transportation,
+ companionship,
+ home-delivered meals,
+ respite care,
+ laundry service, and
+ social day care receive home-care services.

Massachusetts has about 140 Medicaid-certified home health agencies located across the state to provide nursing and home health aide services to Medicaid-eligible residents. Generally, home health services are provided by a local visiting nurse association. Other service providers can be councils on aging, and senior centers that offer social and recreational activities. Nutrition sites, Meals on Wheels, and homemaker-prepared meals generally serve as meal providers for congregate residents.

By agreement between the local housing authority and the various service providers, a congregate sponsor--generally one of the human service agencies--is selected for the project. The congregate sponsor assumes responsibility for service coordination and hires a congregate housing coordinator. The congregate housing coordinator has operational responsibility for ensuring that congregate residents are provided with needed supportive services. Coordinator responsibilities include: screening applicants, determining resident service needs, coordinating delivery of supportive services to residents, support residents in adjusting to congregate housing, and integrating the congregate housing project into the community. A 1984 assessment of of congregate housing in Massachusetts, including state-funded, private, and federal congregate projects, found that the coordinator is the most crucial staff position in congregate housing.

State guidelines have established qualifications for coordinators and have set the minimum number of hours that they must commit to a congregate housing site. A coordinator must have a Master's degree in Social Work with one to two years' work experience or a Bachelor's degree in Social Work or

Human Services with three to five years' experience. In addition, state guidelines require that the coordinator have demonstrated ability to assess support service needs of the elderly and have experience coordinating and integrating community resources.

Costs and Funding

The EOCD and EOEA have reported the following average monthly cost per congregate resident for 1987: shelter, $325; operating, $150; coordinator, $192; and service, $280. The total is $947.

The average monthly state subsidy is $795 per congregate resident. A major cost of the program involves building renovation or construction. Construction is financed by general obligation bonds authorized by the legislature, which authorized an estimated $66 million for FYs 1983, 1985, and 1987. The EOCD reports that interest costs, which are included in shelter costs, range from $88 to $300 per month.

The majority of services are funded through the state-financed Home Care Program. Budgeted at $144 million for FY 1988, it serves an estimated 46,000 elderly a month. Home care costs per congregate resident ranged from $160 to $180 per month. Congregate housing residents with incomes below $16,470 for a single person and $18,339 for a couple are eligible for subsidized home care. The EOEA estimates that about 80 percent of congregate housing residents receive subsidized home care.

Evaluation

A 1984 state evaluation found that congregate housing had met the social goals set for the program. These goals included promoting independence through interdependence, offsetting social isolation, and enhancing residents' well-being. Although the state could not provide any precise data on delayed nursing home admissions due to congregate housing, Massachusetts reports that 11.6 percent of its congregate population moved from nursing homes to congregate facilities. The average monthly cost of congregate care ($947) compares favorably to the average Medicaid rate for nursing home care ($1,260).

The 1984 evaluation concluded that the congregate housing program provides alternative housing for the at-risk elderly, delays their admission into a nursing home, and substitutes for individual public housing units that would be built in the absence of congregate housing. The EOEA reports that the extensive shared living environment permits people to remain in the program longer than if they resided in fully independent apartments. Further, the existence of a statewide home care program enabled congregate projects in rural areas to provide approximately the same level of supportive services as projects located in urban areas. Massachusetts believes that its congregate housing program could be adopted by other states provided that there is an adequate supply of service providers.

Sources

Interviews with Polly Welch, EOCD; Dorthy Altman, EOCD; Jean Multenberry, EOEA; and Edward Blake, DPW.

Executive Office of Elder Affairs. Congregate Housing for Older People: An Effective Alternative. June 1984.

Executive Office of Elder Affairs. Guidelines for the Planning and Management of State-Funded Congregate Housing for Elders. October 1987.

Executive Office of Elder Affairs. Independence through Interdependence. December 1984.

NEW YORK

Overview of Program

New York's Enriched Housing program, begun in 1978, is a state-supported service program established for the frail elderly in existing housing. Under regulations issued by the Department of Social Services (DSS), program sponsors provide or arrange for housing with supportive services to frail elderly, who, because of declining health or functional impairments, are no longer able to live independently. The DSS inspects the ongoing operation of individual Enriched Housing projects to ensure they are in compliance with program regulations.

The program uses existing housing stock, including apartment buildings--public, subsidized, and private--and shared single-family homes. Participants are charged a monthly fee that covers rent and a package of support services. Participants may be private-paying or, if low income, have their monthly fee subsidized by a state supplement to their monthly SSI benefit.

The DSS reports that Enriched Housing projects are developed when support services for the elderly are nonexistent, fragmented, or unavailable to the frail elderly. Enriched Housing sponsors provide participants with support services directly, and existing federal and state service programs are used to the extent that they supplement those services provided under Enriched Housing.

As of 1988, there are 24 agencies sponsoring Enriched Housing projects. These sponsors serve approximately 500 frail elderly residing in 490 units in 44 buildings. Sponsors must be either nonprofit organizations or public agencies and are usually separate from the building managers and owners.

Housing Environment

The Enriched Housing projects involve existing housing and are located in various types of residential settings. About 80 percent of Enriched Housing residents live in public or subsidized senior citizen apartment buildings, with the rest living in private apartment buildings or shared single family homes.

In order to avoid creating an institutional environment in buildings where the Enriched Housing program has been established, program participants may occupy no more than 25 percent of the units. Exceptions to this rule have been granted in situations where a sponsor can demonstrate that a higher proportion of participating units is needed in order to make a project economically viable. The DSS estimates that at least 16 participants are required in order for the project to be fully efficient.

Each program site must have one common area where a congregate meal is served and where recreation activities take place. Sponsors decide on specific living arrangements, which may include shared apartments, shared homes with private bedrooms, and one-bedroom or studio apartments.

Most sponsors have shifted away from shared units, which housed about one-half the program participants in 1982, but represents only about 15 percent of the total in 1988. The major reason for this shift toward independent apartments is resident preference; the majority of residents lived alone prior to joining Enriched Housing and prefer not to share living quarters. A 1982 DSS-sponsored evaluation of the Enriched Housing program found that participants who lived alone in their own apartments were significantly more satisfied with their housing than were those who lived in shared apartments.

DSS regulations require that Enriched Housing sites be located in areas where residents have ready access to medical facilities, shops, senior citizen centers, and public transportation.

Although there is no state funding for new construction, DSS provides development grants for minor building renovations and modifications (e.g., as installation of grab bars), to help facilitate resident independence. These grants can also cover other start-up costs (e.g., salaries, rent, equipment, furnishings).

Target Population and Admission Criteria

Enriched Housing is targeted to adults at least 65 years old who have a level of functional impairment that does not require continuous medical attention but who are not capable of independent living without the basic service package provided in Enriched Housing. DSS regulations define "functional impairment" as disabilities and health conditions that prevent an individual from performing on a regular basis the normal activities of daily life necessary for independent living. Included in this definition are inabilities in regard to one or more of the following: cooking, housecleaning, shopping, and personal care activities.

The project sponsor must hire a program coordinator, who conducts interviews with prospective applicants using a DSS functional assessment form. In addition, applicants must have their physicians complete medical evaluations to assist in determining their suitability for the program.

The functional assessment form provides an overall assessment of the level of services applicants would require and indicates whether the program can meet their needs. It also assists coordinators in setting up a specific service plan for program participants. The form does not generate a numerical measurement of an applicant's ADL or IADL dysfunction.

DSS regulations also list physical and mental characteristics that are inappropriate for Enriched Housing. Included are chronic bedfast, in need of constant medical or nursing supervision, and emotional instability.

The 1982 evaluation of the Enriched Housing program found that the overall impression an applicant made during the interview process was often the basis upon which the admission decision was made. Program coordinators reported that the degree of acceptable frailty was hard to determine but that the preferred applicant fell somewhere between "frail enough to need service" and "frail enough to require near-constant attention." About 5-10 percent of program participants were in residential health care facilities (e.g., nursing homes) prior to joining Enriched Housing.

The 1982 evaluation found that sponsors who followed DSS program standards were generally successful in screening out the most severely health-impaired applicants and concentrating on those elderly with more limited functional impairments who could be helped to remain in the community. The evaluation also concluded that the Enriched Housing population had greater physical frailty than the elderly population at large.

Types of Services

DSS regulations require that each Enriched Housing participant be guaranteed a core package of services that includes:

✦ one daily congregate meal seven days a week and, if needed, assistance with food shopping and preparation of other daily meals and snacks;
✦ weekly housekeeping services;
✦ personal care, including assistance with grooming, bathing, dressing, and taking self-administered medications;
✦ case management, including counseling to facilitate adjustment to the program, meetings to resolve grievances, and assistance to obtain additional services and entitlements;
✦ shopping;
✦ laundry;
✦ periodic heavy housecleaning;
✦ transportation;
✦ leisure activities; and
✦ 24-hour emergency telephone coverage.

The level of use each service is determined by the initial functional assessment and annual reevaluations for each participant.

Service Provision

New York regulations allow project sponsors flexibility in determining staffing necessary for program operation. The DSS emphasizes the key role of the program coordinator, who is responsible for screening applicants, determining the specific level of services for each participant, and overseeing delivery of program services. The program coordinator is employed by the sponsor.

DSS regulations require that coordinators possess a Master's degree in Social Work with at least one year of related work experience or a Bachelor's degree with at least three years

of related work experience. A coordinator must work one and
one-half hours per participant per week for the first 16
participants and one hour per week for each additional
participant. If the coordinator is also the case manager, then
he or she must provide an additional one-half hour of
counseling and case management support per week to each
participant. If the case manager is separate from the
coordinator, the case manager must have a Master's degree in
Social Work, or an undergraduate degree with one to three
years' work experience providing adult services.

DSS regulations require that each sponsor provide a staff
to perform personal care, housekeeping, and meal service
functions totaling at least six hours per resident per week. The
hourly breakdown of each service provided is dependent on the
service needs of each resident. Participant needs that exceed
this six-hour limit may be met from other funding sources,
such as Medicaid.

Program sponsors have the flexibility either to hire on-site
staff or to contract for vendors to perform housekeeping and
personal care services. The daily congregate meal is usually
prepared by a program staff person.

Costs and Funding

The Enriched Housing program provides a subsidy to low-
income participants who are eligible for the state's SSI benefits.
The subsidy mechanism is a special state SSI supplement,
known as Congregate Care Level II. This funding stream also
funds other programs such as Adult Homes for the mentally
disabled. Approximately 75 percent of the 500 Enriched
Housing participants receive funds through the SSI
supplement, and the remainder are private paying.

The monthly fee charged subsidized participants in the
Enriched Housing program and monthly subsidies provided to
them are controlled by the New York State legislature. The
linchpin in this scheme of statutory control is the SSI
Congregate Care Level II rate, which was set by the legislature
in 1988 at $759 for upstate residents and $789 for downstate
residents. In 1987, the figures were $705 and $735,
respectively. This rate and the accompanying regulations

determine the size of the monthly fee and the monthly subsidy payment.

The relationship of the SSI Congregate Care Level II rate, the monthly fee, and the monthly subsidy payment is summarized below. As can be seen, the Level II rate effectively determines the total expenditures and total income of a subsidized participant in Enriched Housing.

Monthly fee = Congregate Care Level II rate - personal allowance

New York subsidy = Congregate Care Level II rate - federal contribution - countable income of participant.

The monthly fee charged program participants is generally an inclusive amount, covering housing, food, and all services. For subsidized participants, the monthly fee is set at the SSI Congregate Care Level II Rate minus a personal allowance. Under the current regulations, the personal allowance must be at least $74, which in effect sets a ceiling on the monthly fee of $685 for upstate residents and $715 for downstate residents.

Project sponsors have discretion to set the personal allowance above the $74 minimum. Currently, the average personal allowance for SSI participants is approximately $100 per month, with a high of approximately $125 per month. The variation in personal allowance among SSI participants results in a parallel variation in the monthly fee.

Project sponsors have authority to impose higher monthly fees on private-pay participants than on subsidized participants. However, DSS indicates that most sponsors charge private-pay participants roughly the same monthly fee as subsidized participants.

All participants at any program site generally pay the same monthly fee irrespective of the level of services that they are using under the Enriched Housing program. This flat fee structure imposes considerable budgetary rigidity on project sponsors, because the level of services provided can vary significantly among individual participants and among projects.

The <u>monthly subsidy</u> received by subsidized program participants is the amount by which their own income (countable income) falls short of the Congregate Care Level II rate. This subsidy has a federal component and a state component. The state component, which is funded out of the New York's SSI budget, currently ranges from $1 to $435 per month, with an average of $350 per month. A subsidized participant is issued a single monthly check that includes all federal and state subsidies to cover his or her Enriched Housing costs.

Based on this $350 average state subsidy per eligible participant, the Enriched Housing program was funded by the state at approximately $1.5 million in 1988. These funds were allocated from the state's SSI budget, which in turn comes out of the state's general funds. Moreover, approximately $150,000 in additional funds is appropriated annually for grants to help cover project start-up costs.

Because the cost of providing services has risen faster than legislative increases in the Congregate Care Level II rate, most sponsors are operating in a deficit position. As of 1988, 22 of the 24 sponsors ran a deficit, estimated at $5 per day per participant. The state has established a special fund to help reduce the sponsors' deficits. In 1988, this fund received approximately $350,000, which covered one-half of the sponsors' deficits.

Evaluation

The DSS-sponsored evaluation of the Enriched Housing program, conducted early (1982) in the program's history, found a high level of unmet service needs among participants prior to their joining the program. For example, about three-quarters of interviewed participants reported that they needed help with getting to their doctors' offices, doing heavy housekeeping, and grocery shopping. Yet only about half the participants had received help with housekeeping and less than half had received help with shopping or transportation.

The Enriched Housing program was effective in meeting these unmet needs of frail elderly--particularly those tasks necessary for daily living. Further, 68 percnet of participants found life easier since their joining the program.

Program coordinators also reported that most participants did not feel stigmatized by being in the program and that other building residents did not know who was and was not in the program. The study concluded that the scattered units approach to the program and discreet project profile maintained at most buildings was generally successful in achieving an integrated atmosphere.

The relatively small number of program sites (44 buildings) established since the program began in 1978 is partly explained by housing provider reluctance to permit introduction of the Enriched Housing program in their buildings. Housing managers generally believe that if residents need support services, they should move out. The DSS and New York's Office for the Aging market the program and encourage participation, but establishment of additional program sites depends on sponsor initiative and housing provider cooperation.

New York's decision to use the SSI to subsidize program participants tapped a large existing funding stream. However, the statutory framework controlling the size of fees and subsidies has drawbacks. The SSI Congregate Living Level II Rate, which determines the fees and subsidy levels, is set periodically by the legislature. Thus, sponsors must work with a relatively rigid fee and subsidy levels to serve an increasingly older program population with increasing service needs. For example, the average age of an Enriched Housing participant rose from 77 in 1982 to 83 in 1988. The fact that 22 of the 24 program sponsors have deficits in large measure reflects the inability of projects to keep pace with rising costs. In addition, the flat fee structure discourages sponsors from tailoring service packages to the particular needs of individual participants.

Sources

Interview with Martin McMahon, Director, Adult Services, Department of Social Services.

Vera Prosper. 1987. A Review of Congregate Housing in the U.S. New York Office for the Aging, Division of Program Development and Evaluation.

Rural Aging Services Partnerships, New York Office for the Aging. 1985. Enriched Housing: A Step-by-Step Program Development Guide.

Third Age Center, Fordham University. 1982. Enriched Housing: A Viable Alternative for the Frail Elderly. An Evaluation of An Innovative Program for Older Persons Sponsored by the NYSDSS. Parts I and II.

OREGON

Overview of Program

Oregon's Assisted Living model was initiated in 1984 to provide support services to the frail elderly and handicapped in independent apartment settings. It is part of an active state effort to provide home- and community-based services in lieu of more costly (and less popular) nursing home placements. A key goal in developing the program has been to provide services up to and including the availability of 16 hours a day of licensed nursing so that even the frailest elderly participants may not only age in place but even finish their lives without having to move to a different setting. The program is unique in the high level of frailty that it is designed to handle, and it embodies a more medically oriented model than most other supportive services programs.

Although the program is operational in three buildings, regulations governing Assisted Living are only now being written. No printed description of the program exists. It has been developed by a consultant to the Oregon Senior Services Division (SSD), working with project sponsors and the state. Assisted Living provides one of three levels of services to the elderly based on level of frailty. All residents of participating buildings must take part in the program and must have some degree of frailty. Residents may be privately paying or paid for by Oregon's 2176 Medicaid waiver funds.

Housing Environment

The buildings currently participating in Assisted Living were newly constructed as elderly housing, with two using state housing finance agency loans and the third commercially financed. Proponents of Assisted Living believe that the model can be made to work in any type of housing--including public housing and rehabilitated buildings--and in other states. A minimum concentration of 20 clients is believed necessary to provide services cost-effectively. Buildings are licensed as residential care facilities.

Despite the model's flexibility in terms of housing settings, the program founders have a strong commitment to maintaining even the most frail elderly participants in independent units, with their own kitchens, bedrooms, and baths. This commitment, combined with the high levels of participant frailty (and often mental dysfunction), would seem to necessitate extensive physical modifications to any building before the program could be implemented. They include grab bars, wheelchair-accessible showers, pull cords, and stoves that have timers or that can be disconnected. Buildings also have congregate dining rooms and central kitchens, but a goal of the model is maintaining flexibility in other settings for bringing in meals or preparing them in the participants' kitchens.

Currently three Assisted Living buildings house and serve 300 residents. All residents participate and, beyond the commitment to independent apartments, there is no attempt to avoid the atmosphere of an institution by limiting the number or proportion of participants or the level of frailty permitted.

Target Population and Admission Criteria

Assisted Living does not prescribe any minimum age and in theory can include disabled persons; Oregon Housing Agency regulations for elderly housing projects set the minimum age at 58. In fact, the average age of program participants is 87. Program operators clearly try to admit only frail elderly in need of assistance. This goal is further evidenced by unofficial estimates that 50 percent of participants use walkers, 40 percent have some problems with incontinence, and 65 percent suffer some level of dementia.

In addition to a physician's evaluation and referral, admission is in part determined by a state-of-the-art functional assessment tool administered by a social worker or Senior Services Division employee. The Client Assessment/Planning Subsystem (CAPS) is a statewide client assessment, case management, and planning process aided by a computerized information instrument. The instrument assesses the functional impairments (mental and physical limitations) of the client as they relate to ADLs, including environmental and situational factors. CAPS is used to determine which of a range of available community-based or nursing home services are most appropriate for particular clients. To qualify for Assisted Living, people must be totally dependent in one IADL or partially dependent in three or more. Further, they should need some assistance daily, including a potential or occasional need for 24-hour on-call attention.

One of the buildings accepts only private-pay clients; the management at another has agreed to accept up to 20 percent of its clients as Medicaid-assisted. This proportion is likely designed to match the Internal Revenue Service requirement of 20 percent low-income residents in pre-1986 buildings receiving tax-exempt bond financing. The third building has some low-income residents but no clients paid for by Medicaid; the church that owns and manages the project assists those in financial need.

Types of Services

Three levels of services are offered. Level one core services (35 percent of clients) include housekeeping, laundry, medication assistance, transportation, three meals per day, counseling, and intermittent nursing; these recipients generally have dependencies in one or two ADLs. Level two (50 percent of clients) includes all core services plus daily personal and nursing services as well as supervision due to cognitive and/or medical impairments; these recipients typically have dependencies in three or four ADLs. Level three (15 percent of clients) adds intensive licensed nursing care for those who are immobile, terminal, and/or aggressively resisting medical care; these recipients are generally dependent in more than four ADLs. Although the program is relatively new, the mix of clients in the different service levels is expected to remain fairly constant due to high (30 percent)) annual turnover in the program and the high proportion of clients who die or otherwise leave the program without reaching the highest service level.

Service Provision

The housing sponsor is responsible for obtaining required supportive services. Except for a single state-employed coordinator/manager primarily responsible for handling eligibility and service plans for Medicaid clients, all staff are employees of the housing sponsor or work on contract from an outside service vendor. In addition to the coordinator and contracted services, it is estimated that 45 staff hours per day are needed to provide for a client population of 20, including one personal care giver on site 24 hours a day.

A sponsor-employed case manager determines along with each client their level of service need, and tailors the nature and frequency of service within each level. Case managers are expected to possess at least a Bachelor's degree in Social Work or a Master's degree in a field such as Gerontology and to complete a brief training session. Case managers also use the state's CAPS instrument to assist in periodic review of services provided to clients.

Costs and Funding

No detailed cost analysis is available for this relatively new program. Clients pay a monthly fee based in part on which of the three service levels they receive. There is some provision for rebates when the complete package of services provided under a service level is not fully needed or used. Estimates from those familiar with the program put the average cost of the program at $1,400 per client per month. For clients covered by state Medicaid waiver payments, the cost is $1,300, with the difference due primarily to the smaller units these clients occupy. Of this total, $500 is for the rent of an average unit, $200 for meals, and the remaining $600 for services. In the present buildings, roughly $100 of the costs of these services si spent on contracted services. Again, the service arrangements are at the sponsor's discretion and are subject to change. Administrative costs account for roughly 10 percent of costs.

Service costs, of course, vary by level of services. Costs for level one services run from $450 to $540 per month per recipient. For level two, they run from $540 to $750, and for level three, from $750 to $1,050.

The $1,300 average monthly cost for assisted clients compares favorably with Oregon's monthly Medicaid reimbursement rates of around $1,350 for intermediate care facilities (ICFs) and $2,550 for skilled nursing facilities (SNFs). For Assisted Living however, Medicaid pays only roughly $700 per client per month after rent is paid and the client's contribution deducted.

Other clients have applied assistance from personal long-term-care insurance and the Veterans Administration Aide-in-Attendance program toward their Assisted Living expenses.

Evaluation

Assisted Living is too new a program to have sufficient basis for meaningful evaluation. It has yet to be implemented in a standard way, and it may better be thought of as a model than as a program. Although an important part of the model is flexibility, forthcoming regulations and a developing base of experience will help translate the model into experience and put it to the test. One problem may be the lack of tangible incentives for housing sponsors to adopt the program or provide a full range of services. In fact, only two of the three projects have implemented the model to anything approaching full extent.

The program does seem to be gaining in popularity. By adopting regulations, officials are upgrading it from trial status to a recognized program. Several congregate facilities are working with the state and consultants to expand their services to become Assisted Living facilities. Moreover, three nursing homes are exploring ways to convert their operations to Assisted Living.

Critics of the program in Oregon have argued that it is not safe enough for participants. The elderly may fall, leave stoves burning, etc. Others object to the mixing of different care levels in the same setting.

It has proven difficult to serve the "near poor" needing Assisted Living. Oregon's Medicaid program covers those with up to 300 percent of the federal SSI income limit, but even so, there is a segment of the population just above these cutoffs that cannot afford to pay for Assisted Living services. Oregon Project Independence (OPI) exists to serve elderly who have been assessed as being at risk of institutionalization and who are not receiving support or services from the state Medicaid agency. The OPI provides less-intensive home care services (averaging around 3 hours per week), but it may include not only such services as housekeeping, escort, and meal preparation, but also personal care and home health agency services. Assisted Living advocates hope to tap into OPI to reach the near poor needing the higher level of support provided by Assisted Living.

There has been a detailed evaluation of Oregon's larger long-term-care system, in which Assisted Living is carving its niche. The state seems to possess a well-developed continuum of care and, with its Client Assessment/Planning Subsystem, a remarkably sophisticated method for screening to ensure that services match needs. Although the 1986 evaluation did not specifically include the new Assisted Living program, there is evidence that screening methods are effective in matching needs and services at all levels.

In Oregon, the alternative care options average one-third of the cost of nursing home care. During the 1980s, the alternative care caseload has grown but the nursing home caseload fell. In May 1986, for example, 74 clients were diverted from admission to nursing facilities and 102 clients living in nursing facilities were relocated to alternative care.

Sources

Interviews and correspondence with: Dr. Keren Brown Wilson, President, Concepts in Community Living and consultant to SSD; Mike Saslow, Special Assistant for Research and Development, SSD; Susan Dietsche, Assistant Administrator for Program Assistance; Larry Dowd, Multifamily Programs Manager, Oregon Housing Agency.

Saslow, Michael G. 1986. <u>Response to Revised SHPDA Review Criteria</u>. Rep.#6. Salem, Oregon: Oregon Senior Services Division, Research and Development Unit.

THE SUPPORTIVE SERVICES PROGRAM IN SENIOR HOUSING

The Supportive Services Program in Senior Housing, sponsored by the Robert Wood Johnson Foundation, seeks to foster the development of innovative approaches to the provision of support services for the frail elderly in public and assisted housing. Through a grant competition for state housing finance agencies (HFAs), the program aims to demonstrate how HFAs, working with housing project owners and managers, can provide and finance supportive services in response to the needs of the frail elderly. Although the program offers considerable promise of identifying feasible models for delivering support services specifically to the frail and at-risk elderly living in public and assisted housing, grants were not scheduled to be made until November 1988 and details of the models proposed by the competing state HFAs were not available when this report went to press. A brief description of the Supportive Services Program itself is possible however.

The program, directed for the foundation by the Florence Heller Graduate School for Advanced Studies in Social Welfare at Brandeis University, will select up to 10 HFA grantees to receive three-year grants of up to $400,000 each. The first year is intended to be a planning phase, with implementation beginning in the last two years. The funds may be used for market analysis, service package design, planning, training, and other activities necessary to implement the supportive services projects, possibly including small initial subsidies for services. The program emphasizes the integration and coordination of existing agencies and service resources. It also emphasizes the importance of partnerships among tenants, management, and service providers. A noteworthy aspect of this program is its use of uncommitted reserve funds from HFAs and local housing developments to help pay for services and supplement state funds, and of community fundraising revenues and client fees.

The selection criteria for the grant competition make it difficult to predict whether the models demonstrated will be replicable in most states. The program will look for agencies with large fiscal resources and experience in integrating a variety of funding sources and in undertaking needs assessments and market research. The states selected will also be those that have strong existing partnerships between housing developments and service providers and active support from both residents and related governmental organizations. In short, although the program will undoubtedly strengthen the service delivery models of progressive states, it is likely to do little to promote supportive services in the less capable, more inexperienced, and challenging states.

Note, appendix D

1. EOCD income ceilings vary from community to community. For the greater Boston area, the income level is $18,144 for a single person and $20,736 for a couple. Residents pay 25 percent of their net monthly income for rent. Income includes Social Security, SSI, pensions, interest, and dividends. In addition, an applicant's total assets may not exceed $15,000.

Appendix E
FEDERAL PROGRAM DESCRIPTIONS

THE NATIONAL DEMONSTRATION OF CONGREGATE HOUSING FOR THE ELDERLY IN RURAL AREAS

Overview of Program

The National Demonstration of Congregate Housing for the Elderly in Rural Areas, developed by the Farmers Home Administration (FmHA) and the Administration on Aging (AoA), was implemented as a demonstration from 1979 to 1983. The purpose of the program was to provide affordable housing and supportive services to elderly and handicapped people living in rural areas. The demonstration consisted of earmarked loans for the construction of congregate housing rental, assistance funds, and supportive services.

The assumption of the program was that congregate housing would improve the quality of life of the rural elderly, particularly those with problems of limited income, poor housing quality, and declining health or functional capability. It assisted them in maintaining or returning to an independent or semi-independent life style and in preventing premature or unnecessary institutionalization as they grew older.

The joint demonstration was formalized between FmHA and AoA in 1979. The FmHA was supposed to choose six diverse rural counties to participate in the program, but 10 sites were eventually selected because of overwhelming interest. The program covered the stages of designing the project, construction of the building, marketing, acceptance of the renters, and the early stage of providing support services. The first project began operating in 1980. Because the program ended in 1983, information on its outcome is limited.

Housing Environment

The FmHA set down relatively broad guidelines for the construction of congregate facilities. The housing was to be economical in construction, it was to be low rise (i.e., not to exceed two stories without elevators), and it could provide space for community rooms, cafeteria, dining, recreation, and other special areas needed by elderly and handicapped residents. The size of the apartment units was to fall within 570 and 700 square feet for one bedroom and 700 and 850 square feet for two bedrooms. Each apartment had to contain a bathroom and complete kitchen facilities.

The average size of the buildings constructed under the program was rather small, with about 30-40 units in total. Each building had unique and attractive features on a rather large site. The buildings basically had one-bedroom units, and approximately 10 percent of the units were for the handicapped.

Target Population and Admission Criteria

The "frail" definition was not strictly described by FmHA. However, because the program's central mission was to provide noninstitutional alternatives for the frail or handicapped elderly, the FmHA mentioned that 20-35 percent of the residents might be elderly or handicapped people requiring some supervision and services. As the result, 19 percent of the tenants of the projects had two or more functional limitations such as activity of daily living or instrumental activity of daily living limitations. Beyond the frailty of physical health, the program covered the people who had lived in an isolated environment and had mental problems and worries. The most usual system for selecting participants was that the housing manager or the service coordinator interviewed and screened them. Some projects set up a formal assessment committee and assessment scales, but not all. There was an income ceiling established by FmHA, which varied by location. The program also intended to achieve a particular mix of tenants- -with 20-35 percent frail, representation of ethnic minorities equal to that in the area's elderly population, and a "good mix" of males and females.

Types of Services

FmHA regulations for congregate housing required that a minimum package of services be provided by every congregate project. These services included: full or partial meal service, with a minimum of one cooked meal per day five days a week; housekeeping for those unable to perform such duties; personal care and services for those needing assistance; transportation and other access to essential services; and social and recreational activities. Grantees were urged to take maximum advantage of existing resources in the community and not to duplicate services already available through other programs. Demonstration funds were expected to support the provision of "limited gap-filling services." Services were provided through reliance on varying combinations of project staff and existing formal and informal community resources. Five of the seven demonstration projects studied had service coordinators paid by demonstration funds. In one site, the area agency on aging (AAA) shared the salaries of the project director and secretary with the owner, and in one site, there was no service coordinator.

Service Provision

FmHA regulations provided that management of a congregate housing project might be done by the owner of the project, a management firm, or an individual agent such as a resident manager. The regulations made no mention of service management as distinct from other management responsibilities. However, AoA indicated that AoA demonstration funds were to be used to support a project director position.

Although there were some similarities, each site adopted a different management structure. The most prevalent pattern involved the location on site of two individuals, one representing the owner as housing manager and the other the AAA manager. The primary coordinators and/or providers of support services were the AAA and other local agencies. The core teams implementing the program were the recipients of federal funds at each location: the developer owner (the FmHA Section 515 local recipient) and the AAA (the recipient of AoA demonstration funds for services). The state Office on Aging and the state and district offices of the FmHA were also involved.

Costs and Funding

The development costs varied among the projects from $1,050,000 to $1,575,000 (1983). The total cost per unit of the demonstration sites averaged $37,781, and the average FmHA mortgage amount averaged $35,998 per unit. Only three demonstration sites completed their developments without exceeding the $1 million loan limit that FmHA had set as a maximum in the original announcement. Most of the supplemental funds for developments over the $1 million mark came from state FmHA allocations. Costs of facility maintenance and operations as well as service coordination and delivery varied. However, because the information was limited at the time of the evaluation, the range was hard to document.

The FmHA would provide for the construction and operation of suitable apartment buildings under the existed Rural Rental Housing Loan Program (Title V, Section 505 of the Housing Act of 1949, as amended). Under Section 505, the FmHA provided rental housing in rural areas for low- and moderate-income families, the elderly, and the handicapped. For the demonstration, $1 million in low-interest Section 515 loans, with a term of 50 years, was earmarked for each demonstration site. In addition, the FmHA set aside "rental assistance" funds to cover all the new units; thus each resident's payment for rent and utilities would be limited to 25 percent of his or her adjusted income, with rental assistance to make up the difference between that amount and the actual rent.

The AoA ensured the provision of supportive services such as meals and transportation under its Model Project authority (Title III, Section 308 of the Older American Act of 1965).

Because AoA's involvement under Model Projects was normally limited to three years, each demonstration site was to be allocated up to $85,000 per year for that period only.

All the congregate housing projects depended on rental assistance for their continued existence. If the rental assistance program were abolished entirely, it was estimated that the majority of the current residents could not continue in the congregate setting.

Evaluation

The evaluation was specially designed to gauge the impact of the program on individuals as an alternative to institutionalization. However, the complete evaluation was not carried out because of an inadequate budget for the survey. Data were collected in seven sites. All the demonstration counties exceeded the U.S. average percentage of the elderly population in 1980. The elderly in the demonstration counties were also more likely to be living below the poverty level than the elderly in the United States as a whole. In most areas, median housing values and rents also fell well below national averages. The towns that the projects served ranged in size from under 1,000 to 10,000 inhabitants.

From the perspective of the program objectives, the project improved the housing situation of the residents served, reduced social isolation, and increased accessibility of supportive services. Concerning the avoidance of institutionalization, there was some transfer of nursing home residents to congregate housing even though the number of cases was limited; in general, little information on this point was developed.

The role of congregate housing in rural areas differs from that in urban communities in two aspects. One is that the housing is expected to respond to the broader needs of rural elderly lacking adequate housing and socialization. In other words, congregate housing in rural communities needs to serve not only the physically impaired but also the mentally deprived. The targeting and screening of participants may not be appropriate if the criteria are the same as those used in urban congregate housing. The second point is the difficulty of g demand. Because of the scarcity of this kind of and facilities for the rural elderly, congregate housing is ⌐ ⌐ted to serve the broader community as a center of the elderly population. On the other hand, the base of demand for this type of housing may not be reliable enough to maintain full occupancy. Selecting project locations is an important factor in ensuring the appropriate number of residents.

The congregate housing program is currently in operation under the rural rental housing program authorized by Title V, Section 515, of the Housing Act of 1949, as amended. The FmHA makes loans to build or renovate housing in eligible rural communities. Although AoA demonstration funds are no longer available, supportive services may be financed by grants from state and area agencies on aging or other appropriate state agencies. The service package should include one meal per day, transportation, housekeeping, personal care, and recreation. Transportation service is a particular necessity for rural congregate housing. Currently (August 1988), the FmHA has made loans to 47 projects, accounting for about 600 units nationwide.

Sources

Interview with Susan Harris, Farmers Home Administration, U.S. Department of Agriculture.

Cronin, R. C., M. J. Drury, and F. E. Gragg. 1983. An Evaluation of the FmHA-AoA Demonstration Program of Congregate Housing in Rural Areas: Final Report. Washington, D.C.: American Institutes for Research.

U.S. Department of Agriculture Farmers Home Administration. 1980. Congregate Housing Financed by FmHA. Washington, D.C.

THE CONGREGATE HOUSING SERVICES PROGRAM (CHSP)

Overview of Program

The CHSP, administered by the Department of Housing and Urban Development (HUD), is based on the premise that the use of appropriate community-based supportive services can help frail elderly and handicapped nonelderly people avoid premature or unnecessary institutionalization. Target populations are the frail elderly and nonelderly handicapped.

The program operates only in HUD-financed public housing projects built and managed by local public housing authorities PHAs and Section 202 sponsored housing.

The CHSP was authorized as a demonstration and funded under Title IV of the Housing and Community Development Act of 1978, also known as the Congregate Housing Services Act of 1978. It was authorized as a permanent program by the Housing and Community Development Act of 1987. In its first fiscal year (1979), the program funded 38 projects. Currently (1988), 60 projects in 33 states serve some 2,000 people. There are 32 sites at public housing and 28 at Section 202 facilities; 45 sites in urban areas and 15 in rural areas; and 51 sites for older persons and 9 for nonelderly handicapped people (American Association of Retired Persons 1988). All but three of the initial grantees are still operating the program in 1988.

Housing Environment

The project must be for the elderly or handicapped and must be either a conventional congregate public housing project or housing for the elderly or nonelderly handicapped owned by a nonprofit corporation and funded under Section 202. The size of facilities that received CHSP experimental funds varied; some had 22 residents, and some had more than 700 residents in a building. The number of residents receiving CHSP services ranged from 10 to 50.

Independent apartment units predominate, although some group homes for nonelderly handicapped are included. All buildings are specially designed to include supportive architectural features (e.g., grabbars in bathrooms, lever door handles, lowered kitchen cabinets, pull cords or other emergency alarm provisions). The project must have a central dining facility.

Target Population and Admission Criteria

Two groups critically vulnerable to premature institutionalization are targeted: the frail elderly (62 years of age and over) and the nonelderly handicapped.

There are no income eligibility criteria other than those that screen the residents of public housing and Section 202 projects.

Vulnerable was originally defined as those who need assistance in at least one activity of daily living (ADL). In 1983, HUD tightened eligibility requirements. The new regulations required grantees to certify in the applicant's files that he or she has an inadequate informal support network and needs assistance in two or more of the ADLs or instrumental activities of daily living (IADLs), one of which must be eating or food preparation. In 1987, the requirements were further revised to three or more ADL and/or IADL limitations appearing on a HUD list, one of which must be eating.

The guideline for CHSP participation in a building was initially set at 20 percent of the residents to maintain an atmosphere of independent living. However, the actual participation rate varied widely on a case-by-case basis, ranging from 10 to 100 percent in group homes for the handicapped.

Types of Services

Program rules required the provision of two meals a day seven days a week for CHSP participants. Meal service was seen as the core service. But in 1987, this requirement was reduced to one meal a day. Additional meals have been retained as optional on a case-by-case basis. Meal service may be purchased by nonparticipants at cost. Services may be contracted out by the site manager.

Trained and supervised homemakers may be used to assist participants, particularly in eating, bathing, grooming, dressing, toileting, and ambulating.

Trained and supervised housekeepers may perform or assist the participants in performing essential household tasks such as cleaning, essential shopping, light laundry, simple home repairs, occasional cooking or preparation of meals in units, and other light work necessary to keep the homes or apartments clean, neat and functional for their inhabitants. Other services necessary to maintain the independence of participants may be provided.

One important condition is that CHSP services not substitute for services already being provided; they must be in addition to these services.

Except meal service, housekeeping/chore service was the most frequently provided service among CHSP sites. Personal care service, shopping assistance, and transportation services were provided by fewer than half of the project sites (Ruchlin and Morris 1985).

Service Provision

Once HUD has approved its grant application, the public housing authority or Section 202 sponsor hires a service coordinator who works with a professional assessment committee (PAC).

Typically, the PAC establishes admissions criteria and reviews resident applications, and the service coordinator provides ongoing case management. Consistent with HUD guidelines, PAC members must include at least one member with a medical background (e.g., doctor, nurse-practitioner, nurse) and a social service professional. The coordinator/manager of the project is also included in the PAC. PAC members are all volunteers and serve without pay.

The CHSP legislation requires public housing authorities and 202 sponsors who receive CHSP grants to establish a cooperative planning process with other community agencies. The AAA and the local agency for the handicapped are specified in the legislation.

Costs and Funding

In FY 1979, the average annual budget for a CHSP site was about $90,000 ($10 million for 37 projects over three years). Between 1979 and 1987, HUD allocated $37 million to CHSP. The current HUD budget is $4,224,000 for 60 projects for 10 months in 1988. The average is about $70,000 per project, but the range is large because the services and number of participants vary from site to site.

In 1982, average CHSP expenditures per participant were $241 in constant 1987 dollars (Sherwood et al. 1985). This figure includes expenditures for meals (14 per week), general administration, housekeeping, personal care, transportation, and social work. Expenditures for meals accounted for a little more than half the total expenditures (Ruchlin and Morris 1985).

The program limits the proportion of expenditures that can be used by the grantee for administrative costs. The participants pay part of the cost of meals and services received. Each project sets its own sliding fee scale. Initially, a scale could be established freely, based on participant income and allowing for a 100 percent subsidy for individuals with extremely low incomes.

At first, HUD encouraged diversity and project-specific tailoring of fee schedules. Some programs had a sliding scale based on participant income and others charged a uniform fee. Some programs established one monthly fee for all meals for all participants; others developed sliding fee scales for individual meals, total number of meals per day, or total number of meals per month.

Many charged only for meals. Even within this one service and within charging mechanisms, there was considerable variation across sites. At sites with a uniform fee for meals, the range was from $10 a month at one site to $100 at another. At sites with a sliding scale, the highest fee at one site ($31) was $3 less than the lowest fee ($34) at another site (Holms 1980).

This diversity of fee schedules was changed in 1987. Flat rate fees are no longer acceptable. All sites must have a sliding fee scale that incorporates a minimum fee of no less than 10 percent of the participant's adjusted monthly income (U.S. Dept. of HUD April 1987).

Evaluation

The CHSP was evaluated by the Hebrew Rehabilitation Program Center for the Aged, which concluded that implementation of the experimental CHSP was generally successful.

According to the performance evaluation, the CHSP experimental program was well targeted in terms of serving the vulnerable elderly. Effective targeting means providing services to those who really need them to maintain their independence (the "vulnerable"), instead of allocating services to those who have no such need (the "nonvulnerable"). Applying the Hebrew Rehabilitation Center for Aged Vulnerability Index, the study concluded that slightly more than one-fourth the 1,706 residents were classified as vulnerable and over 85 percent of the vulnerable residents were provided services. Fewer than one-fourth the remaining nonvulnerable residents were provided services. Overall allocation of services was impressive, although, ideally, only vulnerable residents would receive services. There was a considerable variation in targeting among participating projects. The percentage of nonvulnerable served ranged from 7 to 40. The data suggested that, without special efforts, the provision of services to vulnerable residents could be expected in facilities that were relatively small and that house high percentages of the vulnerable. Viewed from a planning strategy perspective, the study suggested that better targeting to vulnerable residents who constituted a relatively small group within a large facility required additional staff training in outreach methods and the use of assessment procedures (Sherwood, Morris, and Bernstein).

The tailoring analysis looked at the major services provided. It referred to the extent to which CHSP participants received services appropriate to their assessed needs. In determining whether CHSP participants received services appropriate to their needs, the analyses focused on two main issues. One was the degree to which those assessed as having a specific service need received such services, directly through CHSP or other agencies or through informal support resources. The second issue concerned the extent to which particular

CHSP services were provided to people who did not appear to have a specific need for those services.

In many respects, findings were positive from both the tailoring analyses of the three services (meals, housekeeping, and errands). In general, the vast majority of those who needed particular services received them from one source or another; a small minority received services that they did not really need.

Of the six services for which it was possible to determine whether those with no apparent physical functioning need were being served, there were only two--meals (60 percent of the total but only 48 percent of the vulnerable) and chores (50 percent of the vulnerable)--in which 50 percent or more of those with no apparent need were furnished with services.

The service with the highest proportion of those with no functional need was meals. However, it could be said that people with no functional need for meal service could have a social need for such services. Because most sites considered socialization needs in determining eligibility for the CHSP, a meal service evaluation considered only strict physical need and failed to take into account the need for social interaction might be insufficient. Further, the inclusion of greater numbers of residents in the meal program might help reduce the costs of providing the service (Sherwood, Morris, and Bernstein 1984).

To evaluate the impact of the program, the study looked at two groups: selected residents of CHSP buildings (experimentals) and residents of nongrantee PHA and 202 buildings (controls). The major conclusions follow:

♦   The definition of vulnerability used (i.e., deficient in one ADL) was not an accurate measure of vulnerability because it was not likely to identify elderly who were really at risk of being institutionalized. If preventing institutionalization was the primary goal, housing sites that have a small proportion of high-risk elderly (e.g., 25 percent or less) and do not focus on admitting such people even after CHSP-like services become available, were inappropriate choices.

During the first three years of the program, there were no statistically significant differences between the experimental and control groups in the aspect of the avoiding institutionalization. One year later, however, there was a difference in the proportion of experimentals and controls who had spent time in institutions. Overall, about 15 percent of the experimentals had at least one institutional placement, and 23 percent of the controls had such a placement. Thus, for every experimental who experienced an institutional placement, 1.5 controls experienced such a placement.

An institutional placement does not mean permanent residency in an institution. At the end of the study period, as many as 92 percent of the experimentals and 88 percent of the controls resided in a community (i.e., noninstitutional) setting, although three-fourths of the residents in the CHSP building prior to program implementation were not likely to be institutionalized. Within this population over one year, based on natural rates of institutionalization for such people, the number of those estimated to be at risk of institutional placement in the average facility amounts to only 3.5 people, 2.4 of whom would have been functionally vulnerable and 1.1 functionally independent when the program began (Sherwood, et al. 1985). In short, it was hard to say that the CHSP delayed institutionalization.

✦ Quality of life measures examined included mobility, ability to perform daily activities, and ability to care for oneself. There were no differences between the experimental and control groups on these measures. Psychological status measures cover such aspects as life satisfaction and morale. The CHSP has some positive effect on psychological quality of life. A significant effect was found in self-satisfaction. The average experimental CHSP participant was more self-satisfied than the average member of the control group. This finding suggests that the intervention was beneficial with respect to how the individual viewed him/herself.

Participant satisfaction measures included both services and housing. No differences were found with respect to satisfaction with housing. The experimental group was more satisfied with services than the control group.

Social activities included the nature and frequency of social contacts. CHSP intervention neither harmed nor benefited the social activities of the experimental group.

✦   The evaluation sought to determine the extent to which the services provided by the program were supplemental and whether the family and others in the support network stopped providing informal service when formal services were available from the CHSP. In other words, did CHSP services merely substitute for those previously provided informally or through other social service resources and funding sources? Three measures were examined: the level of formal support services received, the level of informal support services received, and the resiliency of informal support services.

Overall, experimentals more hours of formal care than did controls. Experimentals received many more hours of meals and transportation. This information indicates that CHSP did not merely substitute for formal services to individuals received from other agencies, but provided additional services.

Increasing formal service provision did not result in a reduction of informal care. In no area of service was there a significant experimental/control difference in the hours of informal care received. Thus there was no indication of a significant substitution effect.

Eighty-nine percent of both experimentals and controls were receiving at least some informal support services. There were no significant differences in the groups' expectations about continuation of these informal support services.

✦   The maintenance of effort analysis examined the question of whether housing management maintained the services received prior to the building's being funded under other auspices. For effort to be maintained, services cannot be fewer than they would be in the absence of the CHSP. The program did not reduce the number of non-CHSP services, and effort was maintained in the CHSP buildings.

✦   To the extent that it can have positive effects on vulnerable residents in the building, even those who are not participating directly in the program, the CHSP can be considered a potentially cost-saving mechanism for meeting the needs of the frail elderly living in assisted housing. This umbrella effect reduces the use of nonessential long-term-care services.

The major evaluation of the CHSP demonstration program was performed in the early 1980s. After the study, the several program requirements were changed. Specificially, the requirements for eligibility in terms of ADL and/or IADL were strengthened. This change generally means that the targeting became stricter and may result in enrolling only persons really in need and at high risk of institutionalization. In addition, the mandatory meal requirement was reduced so that the tailoring is more flexible. These changes are expected to produce rather different results in effectiveness and efficiency of the current performance of the CHSP program compared with the demonstration program analyzed in this evaluation study.

In addition to the changes noted, the qualifications of the case manager or site coordinators may need attention. The success of the program strongly depends on the site coordinator's ability to handle the program. Basic social work knowledge may be the fundamental requirement for the coordinator. More analysis of qualifications is essential.

A Note on Services Prior to the CHSP[1]

Prior to CHSP implementation, only a minority of CHSP buildings and nongrantee buildings had a package of more than two services. Although almost 20 percent of the houses in the general community had no services, many CHSP houses had at least one nonmedical support service prior to the CHSP (e.g., more than half the non-CHSP and over 40 percent of the CHSP buildings had some type of meal service prior to CHSP implementation).

There was a striking difference in the availability of housekeeper/chore and personal assistance services between CHSP sites and non-CHSP sites prior to CHSP service: 76 percent of non-CHSP sites did not have housekeeper/chore services, compared with 54 percent of CHSP sites; 83 percent of the non-CHSP did not have personal assistance service, compared with 51 percent of CHSP. In the majority of sites with housekeeper/chore and personal assistance services, these services were provided directly by the housing authority/sponsor staff. In one-third of the CHSP sites, these services were contracted out.

The proportion of buildings with social services at CHSP sites and at non-CHSP sites was not substantially different prior to CHSP funding; 54 percent of CHSP sites offered some social services. Social services available in CHSP and non-CHSP were: information and referral, counseling, advocacy, assessment, financial counseling, eligibility determination, legal assistance, and friendly visiting. Social services at most sites were funded and provided directly by the housing authority or sponsor; the housing authority and sponsor were major funders. Other sources of funds include Title XX of the Social Security Act, state, city/county, and Title III C of OAA.

A higher proportion of CHSP than non-CHSP sites had transportation services available prior to CHSP funding but not escort services.

Health services are not funded under the CHSP. But 36 percent of CHSP sites and 30 percent of non-CHSP sites provided health services under other auspices. Services available were: health screening, health education, diagnostic services, and primary care/treatment.

More than half the non-CHSP sites reported that the project manager or other person had responsibility for admissions and assessment; approximately one-third reported that someone had responsibility for service planning, and 42 percent report that someone had responsibility for referral and follow-up. Among housing authorities and sponsors that take on this responsibility, most staff assigned to this function were professionals (i.e., each had at least a Bachelor's degree).

Overall, case management responsibilities were performed at the majority of non-CHSP sites. At sites where any of these functions were carried out, there was little outside agency assistance and housing authority or sponsor professional staff had responsibility.

Note, appendix E

1.   Figures in this section from Holmes (1980).

Sources

Interviews with Aretha Williams and Jerold Nachison, U.S. Department of Housing and Urban Development; and Thelma Millard, Baltimore City Public Housing Authority.

American Association of Retired Persons (AARP). 1988. Congregate Housing Services Program: Questions and Answers. Revised May 22, 1988. Washington, D.C.: AARP.

Holmes, M. B. 1980. A Preliminary Report on the Planning and Implementation Process of the Congregate Housing Services Program. Boston: Hebrew Rehabilitation Center for the Aged.

Ruchlin, H., and J. Morris. 1987. "The Congregate Housing Services Program: An analysis of service utilization and cost." The Gerontologist. 27(1): 87-91.

Ruchlin, H. S., and J. N. Morris. 1985. Service Cost Analysis (Performance Issue 3). Boston: Hebrew Rehabilitation Center for the Aged, Department of Social Gerontological Research.

Sherwood, S. 1985. Executive Summary for the Evaluation of Congregate Housing Services Program. Boston: Hebrew Rehabilitation Center for the Aged, Department of Social Gerontological Research.

Sherwood, S., et al. 1985. Final Report of the Evaluation of Congregate Housing Services Program. Boston: Hebrew Rehabilitation Center for the Aged, Department of Social Gerontological Research.

Sherwood, S., S. A. Morris, and E. Bernstein. 1984. Targeting and Tailoring Performance of the Congregate Housing Services Program. Boston: Hebrew Rehabilitation Center for the Aged, Department of Social Gerontological Research.

U.S. Department of Housing and Urban Development (HUD). 1987a. Request for submission for additional funds. Washington, D.C.: HUD.

____. 1987b. Memorandum, April 1987. Washington, D.C.: HUD.

____. 1986a. Memorandum, February 27, 1986. Washington, D.C.: HUD.

____. 1986b. Request for submission for new funds. Washington, D.C.: HUD.

____. 1983a. Monitoring and Technical Assistance Handbook for the Congregate Housing Services Program (CHSP)--Handbook 4640.1. Washington, D.C.: HUD.

____. 1983b. Request for grant application No. H-12152 Fiscal Year (FY) 1983 Congregate Housing Services Program. Washington, D.C.: HUD.

____. 1983c. Fifth Annual Report to Congress on The Congregate Housing Services Program. Washington, D.C.: HUD.

____. 1982. Request for grant application No. H-10614. Washington, D.C.: HUD.

____. 1981. Second Annual Report to Congress on the Congregate Housing Services Program. Washington, D.C.: HUD.

____. 1980a. News Release. Washington, D.C.: HUD.

____. 1980b. Request for grant application No. H-6340. Washington, D.C.: HUD.

____. 1979a. <u>Request for grant application No. H-6200 Fiscal Year (FY) 1979 Congregate Housing Services Program</u>. Washington, D.C.: HUD.

____. 1979b. <u>HUD News</u>. Washington, D.C.: HUD.

____. 1979c. <u>Request for grant application No. H-6201</u>. Washington, D.C.: HUD.

Appendix   F
DESCRIPTIONS OF POSSIBLE NEW APPROACHES

THE CONGREGATE HOUSING CERTIFICATE PROGRAM

Overview of Program

The Congregate Housing Certificate Program (CHCP), as described in Newman and Struyk (1987), is one of the conceptual models for the provision of both housing and supportive services to the frail elderly. An eligible household would receive a certificate entitling it to occupy an independent unit in a private congregate housing project that provides necessary support services on site. These services would include: limited congregate meals, personal care services, homemaker services, laundry facilities, specialized transportation, and housekeeping. The housing would be a multi-unit project, where units are fully equipped and specially designed to accommodate elderly needs.

Housing Environment

The housing projects and support services would be privately developed, financed, owned, and operated, and they would be encouraged to serve voucher holders as well as households paying the market rate. No predetermined mix of CHCP clients and paying residents has been established.

Potential recipients of CHCP vouchers would be certified by the local public housing authority possibly working with state or local health agencies. Housing assistance income guidelines and the risk assessment tool used for the Congregate Housing Services Program (CHSP) would be applied to determine eligibility. Given a list of approved congregate housing projects, the recipient household would then be responsible for locating and moving into an available unit. Once admitted to a particular site, all further assessment would be done by the housing vendor. It is assumed that both a case manager and medical personnel would work together to tailor the services available to meet individuals' needs.

Target Population and Eligibility Criteria

To be eligible for vouchers, the household would have to meet income criteria for housing assistance, be 62 years of age or older, and be judged at high risk of being institutionalized. Vouchers would be redeemable only in approved projects, as opposed to being used in the household's current home, and the program would endeavor to ensure that a diversity of options was open to certificate holders. At the time of application, households could be either homeowners or tenants. The mandatory condition is that regardless of their ownership status, they must be willing to move into the housing project. This condition is likely to result in an automatic screening out of those at a lower risk of institutionalization and attract those who seriously need the available services.

Types of Services

The services available in the CHCP would include: limited congregate meals, personal care services, homemaker services, self-administered laundry, specialized transportation, and housekeeping. Services would be tailored to clients' needs by an on-site case manager. Services would be provided or contracted for directly by the vendor.

Costs and Funding

The cost of providing housing and support services has been estimated at $954 per month (1987 dollars), assuming that the housing facilities were built in 1985 (Heumann 1985). Assuming that the contribution toward these costs is about 50 percent of the household income and that the income of occupants is the same as that of the "average" elderly recipient of housing subsidies, the monthly subsidy would be $624 (987 dollars) (Newman and Struyk 1987). Although a participant contribution of 50-60 percent of household income has been presumed as a viable rate, it would be only if such a level would not jeopardize the financial stability of the household. The current proposal is for one payment standard. It is possible that this payment might vary with the varying degrees of frailty and need for services.

Evaluation

The total resource cost per month of service at the congregate facility, $954, is higher than the CHSP, $816, because new housing units are being employed exclusively, but it is lower than the cost of the intermediate care facility, $1,431. The cost to the government (subsidy), however, is a little less than that for the CHSP, $624 versus $651, and is considerably below the ICF subsidy of $943. If the tenant's contribution in the CHSP were not set at 50 percent of gross income but kept at the 30 percent rate for housing assistance, the subsidies for the CHCP package and intermediate care would be quite similar (Newman and Struyk 1987).

Comments

The key features of the CHCP are the enhanced opportunity to live in housing with services and the rationalized administrative process and cost of combining housing and supportive services. There has been some recent movement toward using rent supplements (Section 8 Existing housing assistance certificates and housing vouchers) in more supportive living arrangements. Congress authorized two initiatives in 1983 that the Department of Housing and Urban Development is now implementing: the use of rent supplements in both single room occupancy and shared living arrangements (Newman and Struyk 1987). The CHCP could be an important option that avoids the complicated procedures for obtaining and coordinating shelter and supportive services from different public agencies.

A question is whether there are private congregate projects on the market. If there are not, the provider of an existing project is not likely to be willing to offer units to the voucher holders. A small program could easily be accommodated with existing facilities. However, a program of intermediate size might bring some difficulty because suppliers may have to develop new facilities to respond to demand with no guarantee that the demand would be sufficiently large or stable to support a new facility in the long term. Two points suggest that this situation might not present a problem. First, a service might be added to many projects with little difficulty, although some unit modification would generally be necessary. Second, the general evidence on the responsiveness of housing suppliers indicates that supply will be forthcoming if the incentives are right. The CHCP would be considered in conjunction with a program that would stimulate the new supply of specially designed congregate housing (Newman and Struyk 1987).

Sources

Heumann, L. 1985. A Cost Comparison of Congregate Housing and Long-Term Care Facilities in Mid-West. Urbana, Illinois: University of Illinois.

Newman S., and R. Struyk. 1987. Housing and Supportive Services: Federal Policy for the Frail Elderly and Chronically Mentally Ill. Paper no. 2199-)1A. Washington, D.C.: Urban Institute.

LIFE CARE AT HOME

Overview of Program

Life Care at Home (LCAH) is a new long-term-care insurance and service delivery model that combines the financial and health security of a continuing care retirement community (CCRC) with the freedom and independence of living at home. The model was developed by the researchers at Bigel Institute for Health Policy, Brandeis University.

Medicare helps support the expenses of acute illness only; it does not cover care for disabilities resulting from chronic illness. The majority of elderly cannot afford one year in a nursing home. To deal with the financial aspects of long-term care, several models have been developed. Insurance for long-term care is one model; another combines insurance with a service delivery mechanism. Both have as a central feature the pooling of financial risk across an elderly population. Examples of the latter model include CCRCs--which insure and provide health care along with a wide array of nonmedical services such as housing--and social/health maintenance organizations (S/HMOs), which deliver needed health care for a fixed premium. LCAH is a new long-term-care finance and delivery model that combines elements of existing options.

LCAH involves risk pooling for long-term care and provides similar benefits and guarantees of CCRCs, including eventual unlimited nursing home care, to subscribers who continue to live in their own homes instead of moving to a campus. By eliminating the campus or residential community component, program costs are substantially lowered and more individuals can participate. LCAH insures enrollees against the catastrophic costs of long-term-care and provides a case-managed delivery system to ensure access to needed services. LCAH differs from current long-term-care insurance offerings in at least two important ways. First, in addition to financing long-term institutional care, LCAH also manages and provides lower levels of needed care. Second, LCAH places greater emphasis on home care services compared with most long-term-care insurance policies, which cover primarily nursing home care and offer few, if any, in-home benefits. Third, LCAH offers lifetime coverage, compared with the prevailing limit of three to five years of coverage for most long-term care insurance policies. LCAH is also more comprehensive than the S/HMO, which provides limited chronic care benefits.

The first demonstration of this new model is now being developed by a joint venture of a continuing care retirement community (Foulkeways Retirement Community) and a hospital (Jeans Health System) in northwest Philadelphia. The program's start-up is being supported by the Robert Wood Johnson Foundation and the Pew Memorial Trust. The Jeanes-Foulkeways Life Care at Home Program began marketing and enrollment in 1987.

Program participants live in their own homes or apartments. To create a sense of community, the program may develop a centrally located social club and/or health care facility or may simply rely on existing social-community networks.

Target Population and Admission Criteria

The LCAH model will initially enroll on an insurance basis only well elderly up to age 85, excluding those with one or more limitations in activities of daily living (ADLs). There will be an entry assessment similar to what is currently done in CCRCs. Subsequently, eligibility for chronic care services will be determined by case managers who will use a standardized assessment screening tool to determine the applicant's degree of dependence across a number of medical, functional, and mental status factors. When the applicant's eligibility for benefits is determined, the case manager will develop an appropriate care plan that specifies the types and amounts of services the member needs. Individuals who do not meet the entrance criteria may enroll on a fee-for-service basis and receive access to a managed delivery system. The program is expected to appeal to a slightly younger segment of the elderly than campus CCRCs. The majority of entrants will be under age 75, with nearly half between ages 65 and 69. The study assumes an enrollment penetration of about 1 percent, a minimum plan size of 500 members, and a target enrollment of 1,000 members.

Type of Services

The LCAH service package includes two broad categories of services: guaranteed services that will be delivered at no additional cost and brokered services for which members will pay the full cost on a fee-for-service basis. Services are based upon five principles: financial protection, importance to the concept of comprehensive care, cost-effectiveness, marketability, and contribution to the sense of community among enrollees. The guaranteed (insured) services include: the chronic care benefit package, which has skilled and intermediate level nursing care; personal care, home health, and homemaker services; in-home electronic monitoring; respite and day care; occupational speech and physical therapies; and in-home meals. Other services might include: medical/acute care, emergency services and transportation, pharmacy, podiatry, dental care, and eye care. The brokered (noninsured) services (e.g., housing, nonmedical transportation, home maintenance, social and recreational features) will vary, based upon specific market and sponsor characteristics at various LCAH sites.

Service Provision

The package of benefits and services that the LCAH model provides can be developed, marketed, and managed by a single sponsor or by a joint venture of two or more sponsors. The risks associated with managing long-term care are the major hindrance to increasing the long-term-care insurance policies. To control this risk LCAH would use techniques such as specifying appropriate criteria to determine eligibility for enrollment and for benefits, creating benefit limits, using some cost-sharing techniques, and establishing a strong case management system.

Costs and Funding

LCAH, under the several assumptions that the researchers used, is expected to cost between $5,000 and $10,000 in entry fees and between $150 and $200 in monthly fees, depending upon age and marital status at entry and the benefit package. All the entry fee and a sizable portion of the monthly premium are intended to cover institutional care. Monthly premium costs for noninstitutional care services represent only between $40 and $80 of the total amount, depending on the extensiveness of the community-based services covered (Tell, Cohen, and Wallack 1987). It is estimated that a far greater proportion of the elderly can afford LCAH than can presently afford CCRSs. The LCAH model may enroll individuals who do not meet the entrance criteria on fee-for-service basis. The total annual benefit for community-based services cannot exceed what it would cost to care for the member in a nursing home. For example, if it is assumed that annual nursing home costs are $25,000 at a 30 percent copayment level, benefits up to $17,500 annually for community-based services would be guaranteed. Service use beyond that would be paid for by the client on a fee-for-service-basis.

Evaluation

Although the program has not been operated long enough for evaluation, the study mentioned that there existed significant interest in the LCAH concept among elderly consumers because it would insure the costs of long-term care while retaining the right to live in their current homes. LCAH has a market potential of at least 10 percent of all elderly, based on conservative interpretation of interest and eligibility among a randomly sampled elderly population (Tell, Cohen, and Wallack 1987). The critical points, of course, will be the growth rate of chronic illness and long-term-care needs within the insured population.

Sources

Telephone interview with G.F. Malfara, Plan Counselor, Jeanes/Foulkeways Life Care at Home, Philadelphia.

Cohen, M. A., et al. 1987. "The financial capacity of the elderly to insure for long-term care." The Gerontologist 27(4): 499-502.

Jeanes/Foulkeways program brochure.

Tell, E. J., M. A. Cohen, and S. S. Wallack. 1987. "Life Care at Home: A new model for financing and delivering long-term care." Inquiry 24: 245-52.

Tell, E. J., et al. 1987. "Assessing the elderlys' preferences for lifecare retirement options," The Gerontologist 27(4): 503-9.

SOCIAL HEALTH MAINTENANCE ORGANIZATIONS

Overview of Program

The S/HMO demonstration was designed to test the expansion of prepaid coverage of community and nursing home care in a

controlled manner and the linkage of these expa
with a complete acute care system. To accomp
four guidelines were to be followed: a single organizational
structure was to provide a complete range of acute and chronic
care services; a coordinated case management system was to
be used to ensure access to appropriate services; enrollment in
S/HMOs was to include a mix of frail and able-bodied elderly;
and the organizations were to be financed on a prepaid,
capitated basis through monthly premiums from Medicare,
Medicaid, and enrollees.

The four sites (in Brooklyn, New York; Portland, Oregon;
Long Beach, California; and Minneapolis, Minnesota) began
operating in March 1985. As of spring 1987, they had a total
enrollment of more than 11,000 Medicare beneficiaries. All
sites offer all Medicare-covered services plus other expanded
services. Expanded care includes personal care, homemaker
service, day care, respite care, transportation, and institutional
care.

Organizational Models

Two models were developed for the S/HMO demonstration
project. The sites in Portland (Kaiser Permanente) and
Minneapolis (Seniors Plus) are sponsored by an established
health maintenance organization (HMO), thus functioning as a
new benefit program for an existing HMO. The sites in
Brooklyn (Elderplan) and Long Beach (SCAN Health Plan) were
developed as new HMOs by long-term-care organizations.

Although both models provide for case management, its
location in the organizational structure differed. In the HMO-
based model, case management for the S/HMO was separated
from the management of the general HMO programs. In the
new HMO sites where the S/HMO is indistinguishable from the
HMO, case management for all programs was handled as a
unit.

The monthly member premiums for the programs ranged
from $29.50 to $49.00: Seniors Plus, $29.50; Elderplan,
$29.89; SCAN, $40.00; and Kaiser, $49.00.

Problems and Successes

Harrington, Newcomer, and Friedlob (1988a) discuss the organizational and management performance of the S/HMOs over the first 30 months of the demonstration in a paper prepared for the Health Care Financing Administration. They found that the differences in planning, management, and provider arrangements were due to the differences in the sponsoring organizations described above.

The two HMO affiliated S/HMOs became part of organizations that were experienced in delivering hospital and ambulatory care. Although they had limited experience in delivering long-term-care services, they had no difficulty establishing organizational relationships and financial arrangements with long-term providers. Problems with conflicts over strategic planning and marketing arose in the Seniors Plus program in which the sponsor organization, Group Health, Inc., had a competing TEFRA HMO that it considered a more viable product than the S/HMO. (Section 114 of TEFRA, the Tax Equity and Fiscal Responsibility Act of 1982, allows HMOs to enter the elderly market and be reimbursed by Medicare on a prepaid basis.)

The study reported that Elderplan and SCAN, the two new HMO sites, needed extensive staff and financial resources to establish prepaid financing systems and acute and ambulatory care delivery systems. The sponsoring agencies for these sites, long-term-care organizations, contracted for all acute, ambulatory care, and long-term-care services. They provided only administration and case management for the S/HMO projects. Although they had no problems with planning and arranging for the delivery of long-term services, they did have a problem with the planning of acute and ambulatory service delivery.

Services Provided

An S/HMO builds on the concept of a health maintenance organization. Clients of an HMO pay a set fee in advance (called a capitation fee) and have a variety of health services provided for them. The S/HMO extends this model by including long-term-care services. Although the HMOs have the incentive of providing adequate low cost outpatient care to prevent more costly hospitalization, the S/HMOs have the incentive of providing a combination of lower cost outpatient care as well as long-term-care services to prevent high cost hospitalization and institutionalization. The services that are provided by the four demonstration S/HMO sites include: acute and supple mental medical services (medical, dental, optometric, podiatric, mental health, and audiologic services), chronic care services (nursing home care, homemaker services, personal care, respite, adult day health care, and transportation), and case management services.

Limitations are set on the amount of chronic care services available to a member, and a copayment has been required at all sites for all home care. The caps on services were done in one of two ways. At Elderplan and SCAN, a set dollar amount was available to each member for his or her use of either home/community care or nursing home care services or for a combination of the two. At Elderplan, this amount was $6,500 per year and at SCAN it was $7,500. Kaiser and Seniors Plus separated their community and nursing home caps, although they set a limit on the overall use of both services, Kaiser was $12,000 per year and Seniors Plus was $6,250 per year. Copayments vary by site as well: Elderplan, $10 per visit; Kaiser, 10 percent of charges; SCAN, $5 per visit; and Seniors Plus, 20 percent of charges.

Enrollment and Targeting

Controlling for a Case Mix

When the S/HMO project was developed, it was recognized that because the chronic care benefits of the program are not offered within the competing Medicare supplement market, there was a good possibility that the program might be especially attractive to the already disabled population. Financing for chronic care benefits in S/HMOs comes from private premiums and savings on hospital services. Therefore the S/HMOs need to enroll a membership that is no more impaired than a cross-section of the aged population if they are to be financially viable operations.

With the intent of keeping the S/HMO population from becoming over represented by severely disabled persons, the Health Care Financing Administration agreed to allow the demonstration sites to "queue" their applicants according to their self-reporting of disability status. Quotas were established using national and regional data on the prevalence of severe and moderate disability. Severe and moderate disability was based on answers to questions on the application. Sites were allowed to close enrollment to the severely impaired if proportions exceeded 4-5 percent of new participants. For the moderately disabled, they could close enrollment if proportions exceeded 10-17 percent. People who were closed out were placed on waiting lists within the different queue categories. Although none of the sites ended up queuing for the moderately impaired group, all sites except for Kaiser queued for the severely disabled.

Greenberg et al. (1988) estimated the impact of queuing by looking at the proportions of severely impaired clients and the potential proportions of this group if all those in the queue had been enrolled. Each of the sites that chose to queue clients showed different results: Elderplan would have increased the ratio of severely disabled from 6.3 percent to 16.5 percent, Seniors Plus from 5.7 percent to 10.1 percent, and SCAN from 7.9 percent to 8.5 percent. Although these increases differ by site, the general impact of queuing is to decrease significantly the severely disabled population enrolled and thus keep the costs of chronic care benefits in control.

Eligibility Criteria

Although the S/HMOs all followed the same basic screening and assessment procedures, there were no standard eligibility criteria set. Leutz et al. (1985) presented two positions that came out of discussions on eligibility and targeting when the project was first being developed. The topic was whether to limit expanded (chronic) care services to the severely impaired or to include the moderately impaired in the group receiving these benefits. One position was that the inclusion of the moderately impaired allowed for early intervention that could delay, if not prevent, functional decline, thereby keeping future costs of hospitalization or institutionalization at a minimum. The other position was that given the limited S/HMO budget for expanded services, it could be wiser to limit these services to the most severely impaired elderly population. Because the sites were paid a higher reimbursement rate for those clients that were nursing home certifiable (NHC), it was logical to link eligibility for chronic care services partially to NHC status. Although each site developed its own eligibility criteria for receipt of expanded care benefits, they all did use NHC status in some capacity. Three models were used: (1) strictly limiting expanded care benefits to NHC members (Kaiser and Elderplan), (2) providing expanded care to those who are NHC eligible as well as to the moderately disabled (SCAN), and (3) using the NHC eligibility, but allowing for exceptions based on the judgment of case managers and the directors (Seniors Plus).

<u>Enrollment</u>

The initial enrollment goal per site was 4,000 clients in the first 12-18 months. The goal was set this high to provide for both an adequate sample size of all groups in the case mix, and an enrollment level at which sites were expected to break even on their costs. As of December 1986 (21 months), the enrollment at the four sites was as follows: Elderplan, 2,571; Kaiser, 4,305; SCAN, 2,062; and Seniors Plus, 1,688 (Greenberg et al. 1988). Kaiser was the only program to reach an enrollment goal of 4,000. Greenberg also explains that the break-even point for the two sites that formed new HMOs, Elderplan (5,600) and SCAN (3,900), were higher than the point for Seniors Plus (1,850), which was associated with an existing HMO.

Several studies have presented possible explanations for the low enrollment in S/HMOs as follows (Greenberg et al. 1988; Harrington et al. 1988a; Rivlin and Wiener 1988):

1. Many elderly mistakenly believe that Medicare, Medicare supplemental insurance, and the TEFRA

HMO policies provide chronic care benefits. If this were true, it would not be worth it to them to pay the extra cost for S/HMO coverage.

2. Although sites were permitted to limit the number of impaired clients, they did not advertise that fact. Potential clients who waited until they were disabled to apply were often closed out of the programs.

3. Sponsorship by long-term-care organizations may have negatively affected the perceptions of unimpaired Medicare beneficiaries who identified these S/HMOs with chronic illness, nursing homes, and dependency.

4. The elderly are reluctant to change their personal physicians and to give up their freedom to choose providers. This feeling was at times compounded by the limited number of physicians available to program participants and the fact that some of the programs had their acute health care services in hospitals in areas less desirable to the client population.

5. One of program's physician groups did not support the S/HMO concept because the capitation rates were so low. These physicians were known to be discouraging their patients from enrolling in the S/HMO program.

6. The patient premiums were higher than for the HMO competition. Seniors Plus had a particularly hard time marketing its program, given the difference between its TEFRA HMO program's and its S/HMO premiums and its limited marketing and advertising resources and approaches.

Harrington, Newcomer, and Friedlob (1988a) state that the success or failure of the S/HMO enrollment appears to be a function of the ability of these programs to compete with other HMOs as opposed to whether potential clients were offered the choice of a high-option chronic care health plan and rejected it. Greenberg et al. (1988) point out that the early experience of S/HMOs parallels that of commercial carriers of long-term-care insurance.

This same study also looked at the Medicaid enrollment in S/HMOs. Initially, it was planned that 12-20 percent of the enrollees would be eligible for Medicaid. These expectations were too high. As of December 1986, the proportion of Medicaid clients was: SCAN, 10.7 percent; Elderplan, 4.1 percent; Kaiser, 2.4 percent; and Seniors Plus, 1.3 percent. Hypotheses for such a low Medicaid enrollment include: less attention paid to marketing to this smaller segment, difficulties in marketing through the welfare system, and the options that Medicaid recipients already have for long-term-care benefits.

Case Management

The role of the case managers in the S/HMO demonstration sites is to coordinate the comprehensive institutional and community-based long-term-care services that make up the chronic care benefit package. In doing so, they are in contact with acute care providers, informal caregivers, and non-S/HMO service providers (e.g., legal help, social security, housing, meal programs).

The organizational structure of the S/HMO had an impact on the role of the case managers. The two sites that were initially HMO affiliated left the responsibility and control over acute care with the HMO professionals. The sites developing their own HMOs assigned part of the utilization review and discharge planning responsibilities to the case mangers of the S/HMOs.

A large part of the case managers' role, as discussed by Rivlin and Weiner (1988), is to control chronic care costs. This job is accomplished by: encouraging substitution of in-home care for nursing home care, encouraging substitution of less expensive unskilled home help for relatively expensive skilled medical home care services, helping to avoid extended hospital stays for long-term-care patients who no longer have acute care needs, and ensuring that the use of nursing home and home care services is not expensive.

Future Enrollment

Using the Brooking-ICF Long Term Care Financing Model to evaluate potential effects of widely implementing S/HMOs, Rivlin and Wiener (1988) predict an increase in membership between 1986 and 2020. By 2016-2020, 26 percent of the elderly aged 67 and over would be enrolled and pay annual premiums of $887 (1987 dollars) if S/HMOs were widely available. The long-term-care benefits should reduce Medicaid expenditures. By 2016-2020, Medicaid home health expenditures would decrease 8 percent, and Medicaid home health expenditures would decrease 23 percent. This latter decrease reflects the extensiveness of benefits and higher costs of nursing home care. They also predict that the number of Medicaid nursing home patients would decline 6 percent in 2016-2020 from the 1986 base.

Costs and Funding

Revenues for all S/HMO sites came from a variety of sources. Although amounts varied by site, the sources were relatively consistent: premiums, copayments, Medicare-adjusted average per capita costs (AAPCC), Medicaid capitation, interest, and other miscellaneous sources. In general, the largest share of total revenue came from the Medicare AAPCC payments (45-83 percent), and the next largest share came from premiums (11-19 percent).

Harrington, Newcomer, and Friedlob (1988b) examined the financial success of the S/HMOs during the first 24 months of the project. Success was defined as providing S/HMO services while controlling use and expenditures to ensure the financial viability of the organization. Generally, all sites, except for Kaiser, overestimated their total revenues due to lower Medicare and Medicaid enrollments than were expected. The extensive marketing needs had not been anticipated, and these costs were higher than expected as sites attempted to reach their enrollment goals.

The high service costs for the two S/HMOs that developed their own HMOs were related to the high acute and ambulatory use at those sites. The two HMO affiliated S/HMOs were better able to control costs, using their experience in developing appropriate budgets. Table 5.1 in the text compares the net gains or losses for 1985 and 1986.

The losses shown were not unexpected, although they were larger than had been anticipated. According to Greenberg et al. (1988), the sources of the sites' losses were found primarily in high marketing and sales budgets and administration that had not reached economies of scale, as opposed to stemming from the scope of benefits or inability to manage services. As the models are refined and developed, it is possible that these losses will diminish. For new sites to be developed without incurring such large losses, a more detailed look at the specific costs to the program as they relate to the organizational models is necessary. It has been suggested by Greenberg et al. (1988) and Harrington, Newcomer, and Friedlob (1988b) that the more financially viable model may be that in which long-term services are added to an existing HMO. It is important to keep in mind that the initial S/HMO losses were not too different from the experiences of earlier HMOs.

A point made in one evaluation (Harrington, Newcomer, and Friedlob 1988b), is that the two sites not initiated in an established HMO had a more difficult time planning and arranging for the delivery of acute and ambulatory service delivery. Although they were eventually able to work out the difficulties, a point can be made that it cannot easily be assumed that health care organizations and long-term-care organizations can easily begin to provide a mixture of these services. It is with caution that housing programs should begin to look at providing a wide array of long-term-care and health services.

However, it is feasible that people living in publicly assisted housing could use the S/HMO programs. Although Medicaid clients are eligible for the S/HMO services, their enrollment has been low. A special targeting effort to include a large group of the elderly assisted housing population would provide the opportunity for evaluating the costs and benefits of using an S/HMO or S/HMO-like model with a publicly assisted population group.

Sources

Greenberg, et al. 1988. "The Social HMO Demonstration: Early Experience." Health Affairs 7(2): 66-79.

Harrington, C., R. Newcomer, and A. Friedlob. 1988. Medicare Beneficiary Enrollment in S/HMOs. San Francisco: University of California, Institute for Health and Aging.

Harrington, C., R. Newcomer, and A. Friedlob. 1988b. Social/Health Maintenance Organization Financial Performance during the First Two Years of Operation. San Francisco: University of California, Institute for Health and Aging.

Harrington, C., R. Newcomer, and A. Friedlob. 1988b. Social/Health Maintenance Organization and Management. San Francisco: University of California, Institute for Health and Aging.

Leutz, W., et al. 1988. "Targeting Expanded Care To the Aged: Early SHMO Experience. The Gerontologist 28(1):4-17.

Leutz, W., et al. 1985. Changing Health Care for an Aging Society. Lexington, Mass.: Lexington Books.

Newcomer, R., C. Harrington, and A. Friedlob 1988. Health Plan Awareness and Selection by Medicare Beneficiaries. San Francisco: University of California, Institute for Health and Aging.

Rivlin, A., and J. Wiener. 1988. Caring for the Disabled Elderly: Who Will Pay? Washington, D.C.: Brookings Institution.

Yordi, C. 1988. Case Management in the Social Health Maintenance Organization Demonstrations. San Francisco: University of California, Institute for Health and Aging.

Appendix G
ADL AND IADL DEFINITIONS

Support services programs typically include in their eligibility requirements some need for assistance in activities of daily living (ADLs) or instrumental activities of daily living (IADLs). The National Long-Term Care Survey defines ADLs and IADLs in a way similar to many state programs. As such, ADLs include: transfer, mobility, dressing, bathing, toileting, and eating. IADLs include: heavy housework, light housework, laundry, preparing meals, shopping for groceries, getting around outside, going places beyond walking distance, managing money, and making telephone calls. The minimum number of ADLs or IADLs required for eligibility varies, as does the stringency in assessing the need for assistance.

The Congregate Housing Services Program in the Department of Housing and Urban Development (HUD) uses a condensed list of ADLs and IADLs. HUD now places upper and lower brackets on the eligible level of need, requiring that participants need assistance in three or more of the following ADL/IADL categories, one of which must be in eating or food preparation:

1. <u>Eating</u>: may need assistance with cooking, preparing, or serving food, but <u>must</u> be able to feed self;

2. <u>Bathing</u>: may need assistance with getting in and out of the shower or tub, but <u>must</u> be able to wash self;

3. <u>Grooming</u>: may need assistance with washing hair but <u>must</u> be able to take care of personal appearance;

4. <u>Dressing</u>: <u>must be able</u> to dress self but may need occasional assistance; and

5. <u>Transferring</u>: may need assistance in doing housework, grocery shopping, or laundry, but <u>must</u> be mobile; does not prohibit persons in wheelchairs or those requiring mobility devices.

Source

U.S. Department of Housing and Urban Development (HUD). 1983. <u>Monitoring and Technical Assistance Handbook for the Congregate Housing Services Program (CHSP)--Handbook 4640.1.</u> Washington, D.C.: HUD.

Appendix H
NOTES ON A "UNIFIED PAYMENT SYSTEM"

How would a unified funding system work when, for example, the federal government funded housing services and the state funded support services? Our idea is for the states to transfer the necessary funds to HUD for dispersal to the projects. Annually, HUD would estimate, based on program data, the number of frail elderly to receive subsidized supportive services and inform the states, who would in turn make the necessary payment to HUD. At the end of the year, there would be a reconciliation based on actual usage. The provider would deal with a single agency and receive payments from a single source.

An important question concerns whether the states in effect lose control of their funds by participating in this process. This need not be the case. There are at least three ways for the states to have a powerful role in determining the content and administration of such a program.

1. The package of services to be provided would be decided jointly by the state and federal government, as part of the process for HUD to commit the incremental units and states to commit funding for services. Because the states are paying for the services, some latitude could be possible. The on-site case managers would have primary responsibility for making tailoring decisions. Presumably, there would be standard guidelines across states for admission into the program.

2. While HUD would have the primary oversight responsibility through the Area Office network, state or local social service agencies should fully participate with HUD in conducting management reviews. The state agencies would have primary responsibility for reviewing delivery of supportive services, and recommending corrective actions where necessary; if

projects were ultimately judged incapable of providing services competently, the state would have the right to withdraw services from the project. (But HUD/state action would be taken to help the tenants find other appropriate housing.) Results of management and financial reviews conducted by HUD would be shared with the germane state agency.

3. An Advisory Group drawn from among the states participating in the program would be created to review proposed modifications in HUD regulations governing the program, to ensure that the states' interests and views were fully considered in this process.

Ways could also be developed to ensure that states "get credit" with clients for providing the services. Appropriate posters could be placed in projects, copayment notices could contain a small statement that the cost of services are partly paid by the state, etc.

REFERENCES

American Association of Retired Persons (AARP). 1988. Congregate Housing Services Program: Questions and Answers, Revised May 22, 1988. Washington, D.C.: AARP.

____. 1986. Options for the expansion of supportive housing services. Memorandum. AARP.

____. 1984. Housing Options for Older Americans. AARP.

____. N.d. Supportive housing. Memorandum. AARP.

Anthony, A. S. 1984. "Statement." In Sheltering America's Aged: Options for Housing and Services, Hearing before the Special Committee on Aging, United States Senate. Washington, D.C.: U.S. Government Printing Office.

Binstock, H. 1987. "Title III of the Older Americans Act: An Analysis and Proposal for the 1987 Health Organization." The Gerontologist 27(3): 259-65.

Brooks, E. 1988. A Survey of Housing Trust Funds. Washington, D.C.: Center for Community Change.

Burwell, B. 1986. "Home and Community-Based Care Options under Medicaid." In Affording Access to Quality Care. Washington, D.C.: National Governors' Association.

Cantor, M., and R. Donovan. 1982. Enriched Housing: A Viable Alternative for the Frail Elderly. New York: Fordham University, Third Age Center.

Center for the Study of Social Policy (CSSP). 1988. Completing the Long-Term Care Continuum: An Income Supplement Strategy. Washington, D.C.: CSSP.

Coalition on Human Needs (CHN). 1986. Block Grants: Beyond the Rhetoric. Washington, D.C.: CHN.

Cohen, M., et al. 1987. "The Financial Capacity of the Elderly to Insure for Long-Term Care." The Gerontologist 27(4): 494-502.

Cohen, M., E. Tell, and S. Wallack. 1986. The Client Related Risk Factors of Nursing Home Entry among Residents of Six Continuing Care Retirement Communities. Waltham, Mass.: Brandeis University, Heller School.

Connecticut. Commission on Housing. 1985. Congregate Housing Study Committee. Hartford.

Cronin, R. C., M. J. Drury, and F. E. Gragg. 1983. An Evaluation of the FmHA-AoA Demonstration Program of Congregate Housing in Rural Areas, Final Report. Washington, D.C.: American Institutes for Research.

Duke University Center for the Study of Aging and Human Development. 1978. Multi-dimensional Functional Assessment: The OARS Methodology, A Manual. Durham, N.C.: Duke University, 2d edition.

Eastbaugh, S. 1987. Financing Health Care. Boston: Auburn House Publishing Company.

Gaberlavage, G. 1987. Social Services to Older Persons under the Social Services Block Grant. Washington, D.C.: Public Policy Institute, American Association of Retired Persons.

Greenberg, J., et al. 1988. "The Social HMO Demonstration: Early Experience." Health Affairs 7(2): 66-79.

Greenberg, J., W. Leutz, and R. Abrams. 1985. "The National Social Health Maintenance Organization Demonstration." Journal of Ambulatory Care Management 8(4): 32-61.

Gutkin, C., et al. 1987. The Relationship of Housing and Case-Managed Home Care to the Substitution of Formal for Informal Care. Boston: Hebrew Rehabilitation Center for the Aged.

Hancock, J., ed. 1987. Housing the Elderly. New Brunswick, N.J.: Rutgers University.

Harrington, C., R. Newcomer, and A. Friedlob. 1988a. Medicare Beneficiary Enrollment in S/HMOs. San Francisco: University of California, Institute for Health and Aging.

_____. 1988b. Social/Health Maintenance Organization Financial Performance during the First Two Years of Operation. San Francisco: University of California, Institute for Health and Aging.

_____. 1988c. Social/Health Maintenance Organization and Management. San Francisco: University of California, Institute for Health and Aging.

Heumann, L. 1988. "Assisting the Frail Elderly Living in Subsidized Housing for the Independent Elderly: A Profile of Management and its Support Priorities." The Gerontologist 28(5): 625-31.

_____. 1987. The Retention and Transfer of Frail Elderly Living in Independent Housing. Urbana, Ill.: University of Illinois, Housing Research and Development Program (UI).

_____. 1985. A Cost Comparison of Congregate Housing and Long-Term Care Facilities in the Mid-West. Urbana, Ill.: UI.

Holmes, M. B. 1980. A Preliminary Report on the Planning and Implementation Process of the Congregate Housing Services Program. Boston: Hebrew Rehabilitation Center for the Aged.

Holshauser, W., and F. Waltman. 1988. Aging in Place: The Demographics and Service Needs of Elders in Urban Public Housing. Boston: Citizens Housing and Planning Association.

Housing and Development Reporter. 1987a. "HUD will bar mandatory meals programs...." 14(38): 779.

____. 1987b. "Mandatory meal charges may be imposed...." 15(18): 342-3.

Joint Committee Print, Senate Committee on Banking, Housing and Urban Affairs, and House Committee on Banking, Finance and Urban Affairs. 1987. A New National Housing Policy. Submissions by interested organizations.

Kane, R. A., and R. L. Kane. 1981. Assessing the Elderly: A Practical Guide to Measurement. Lexington, Mass.: Lexington Books.

Kaye, W. 1987. Dignity, Independence, and Cost-Effectiveness: The Success of the CHSP. Testimony to Subcommittee on Housing and Consumer Interest. Bryn Mawr, Penn.: Bryn Mawr College.

Kemper, P. 1988. "The Evaluation of the National Long-Term Care Demonstration: Overview of the Findings." Health Services Research 23(1): 161-74.

Leutz, W., et al. 1988. "Targeting Expanded Care to the Aged: Early SHMO Experience." The Gerontologist 28(1): 4-17.

____. 1985. Changing Health Care for an Aging Society. Lexington, Mass.: Lexington Books.

Maine. Bureau of Maine's Elderly. 1984. A Report on Maine's Congregate Housing Program. Augusta.

Manton, K., and K. Liu. 1987. "The 1982 and 1984 National Long-Term Care Surveys: Their Structure and Analytic

Uses." Paper presented at National Conference on Long-Term Care Data Bases. 21-22 May. Washington, D.C.

Massachusetts Department of Elder Affairs. 1984. Congregate Housing for Older People: An Effective Alternative. Boston.

McDowell, I., and C. Newell. 1987. Measuring Health: A Guide to Rating Scales and Questionnaires. New York: Oxford University Press.

Meyer, J. W., and A. Speare, Jr. 1985. "Distinctively Elderly Mobility: Types and Determinants." Economic Geography 61(1): 79-86.

Mollica, R., J. Moltenbrey, and J. Dionne. 1987. Guidelines for the Planning and Management of State-Funded Congregate Housing for Elders. Boston: Executive Office of Elders Affairs.

Morris, J., et al. 1987. "Housing and Case Manager Home Care Programs and Subsequent Institutional Utilization." The Gerontologist 27(6): 788-96.

Morris, J., et al. 1986. Housing and Case Manager Home Care Programs and Subsequent Institutional Utilization. Boston: Hebrew Rehabilitation Center for the Aged.

Nachison, J. 1985. "Congregate Housing for the Low and Moderate Income Elderly--A Needed Federal State Partnership." Journal of Housing for the Elderly (Fall/Winter): 65-80.

National Center for Health Statistics. 1987. "Aging in the Eighties: Functional Limitations of Individuals Age 65 Years and Over." Advance Data from Vital and Health Statistics no. 133.

National Committee on Vital Health and Statistics, Subcommittee on Long-Term Care. 1988. Photocopy.

National Institutes of Health. 1987. Geriatric Assessment Methods for Clinical Decisionmaking 6(13).

Nenno, M. K., and G. Colyer. 1988. New Money and New Methods: A Catalog of State and Local Initiatives in Housing and Community Development. Washington, D.C.: National Association of Housing and Redevelopment Officials.

Nenno, M. K., J. S. Nachison, and E. Anderson. 1985. "Support Services for the Frail Elderly or Handicapped Persons Living in Government-Assisted Housing: A Public Policy Whose Time Has Come." Public Law Forum 5(2): 69-84.

Netting, F., and C. Wilson. 1987. "Current Legislation Concerning Life Care and Continuing Care Contracts." The Gerontologist 27(5): 645-51.

Newcomer, R., C. Harrington, and A. Friedlob. 1988. Health Plan Awareness and Selection by Medicare Beneficiaries. San Francisco: University of California, Institute for Health and Aging.

Newman, S. 1986. Citizens' Housing and Planning Association Study of the Elderly in Public Housing: Review Prepared for the Robert Wood Johnson Foundation. Baltimore: Johns Hopkins Institute for Policy Studies. Photocopy.

Newman, S. J., and A. B. Schnare. 1988. Subsidizing Shelter. Washington, D.C.: Urban Institute Press.

Newman, S. J., M. Rice, and R. Struyk. 1987. Overwhelming Odds: Caregiving and the Risk of Institutionalization. Washington, D.C.: Urban Institute.

Newman, S., and R. Struyk. 1987. Housing and Supportive Services: Federal Policy for the Frail Elderly and Chronically Mentally Ill. Washington, D.C.: Urban Institute.

Peterson, G., et al. 1986. The Reagan Block Grants. Washington, D.C.: Urban Institute Press.

Pollak, P., C. Higgins, and C. Decker. 1985. Enriched Housing: A Step-by-Step Program Development Guide. Albany, N.Y.: Office for the Aging.

Prosper, V. 1987. A Review of Congregate Housing in the United States. Albany, N.Y.: Office for the Aging.

Rabin D. L., and P. Stockton. 1987. Long-Term Care for the Elderly. New York: Oxford University Press.

Rivlin, A., and J. Wiener. 1988. Caring for the Disabled Elderly: Who Will Pay? Washington, D.C.: Brookings Institution.

Robert Wood Johnson Foundation (RWJH). 1988. Supportive Services Program in Senior Housing: Call for Proposals. Princeton, New Jersey: RWJH.

Ruchlin, H., et al. 1987. Expenditures for Institutional and Community-Based Services by a Cross-Section of Elderly Living in the Community. Boston: Hebrew Rehabilitation Center for the Aged.

Ruchlin, H., and J. Morris. 1987. "The Congregate Housing Services Program: An Analysis of Service Utilization and Cost." The Gerontologist 27(1): 87-91.

____. 1985. Service Cost Analysis (Performance Issue 3). Boston: Hebrew Rehabilitation Center for the Aged, Department of Social Gerontological Research.

Shapiro, E., and R. Tate. 1988. "Who Is Really at Risk of Institutionalization?" The Gerontologist 28(2): 237-45.

Sherwood, S. 1985. Executive Summary for the Evaluation of Congregate Housing Services Program. Boston: Hebrew

Rehabiltiation Center for the Aged, Department of Social Gerontological Research.

Sherwood, S., S. A. Morris, and E. Bernstein. 1984. Targeting and Tailoring Performance of the Congregate Housing Services Program. Boston: Hebrew Rehabilitation Center for the Aged, Department of Social Gerontological Research.

Sidor, J. 1988. State Housing Initiatives: The 1988 Compendium. Washington, D.C.: Council of State Community Affairs Agencies.

____. 1987. Developments in Aging: 1987. Washington, D.C.: Government Printing Office.

____. 1984. Sheltering America's Aged: Options for Housing and Services. Washington, D.C.: U.S. Government Printing Office.

Stegman, M. 1987. Nonfederal Housing Programs: How States and Localities Are Responding to Federal Cutbacks in Low-Income Housing. Washington, D.C.: Urban Land Institute.

Struyk, R., M. Turner, and M. Ueno. 1988. Future U.S. Housing Policy: Meeting the Demographic Challenge. Washington, D.C.: Urban Institute Press.

Tell, J., et al. 1987. "Assessing the Elderly's Preferences for Lifecare Retirement Options." The Gerontologist 27(4): 503-9.

Tell, J., and S. Wallack. 1987. "Life Care at Home: A New Model for Financing and Delivering Long-Term Care." Inquiry 24(Fall): 245-52.

Thielen, R., R. Mollica, and B. Ryther. 1987. Congregate Housing. Washington, D.C.: Council of State Housing Agencies and National Association of State Units on Aging.

Thielen, R., M. Tiven, and B. Parkoff. 1987. Adding Services to Existing Buildings. Washington, D.C.: Council of State Housing Agencies and National Association of State Units on Aging.

Tiven, M., and B. Ryther. 1986. State Initiatives In Elderly Housing: What's New What's Tried and True. Washington, D.C.: Council of State Housing Agencies and National Association of State Units on Aging.

U.S. Bureau of the Census. 1985. Receipt of Selected Noncash Benefits: 1985. Current Population Reports, ser. P-60, no. 155.

____. 1985. Characteristics of Households and Persons Receiving Selected Noncash Benefits: 1984. Current Population Reports, ser. P-60, no. 150. Washington, D.C.

U.S. Congress, Select Committee on Aging. 1987. Dignity, Independence, and Cost-Effectiveness: The Success of the Congregate Services Program. Washington, D.C.: Government Printing Office.

U.S. Congress, Senate. Special Committee on Aging. 1987. Developments in Aging. Washington, D.C.: Government Printing Office.

____. 1986. Developments in Aging. Washington, D.C.: Government Printing Office.

____. 1984. Sheltering America's Aged: Options for Housing and Services. Washington, D.C.: Government Printing Office.

U.S. Department of Health and Human Services (HHS), Health Care Financing Administration. 1987. Program Statistics--Analysis of State Medicaid Program Characteristics, 1986. Washington, D.C.: HHS.

____. N.d. 1982 National LTC survey: Methods and procedures. Photocopy.

U.S. Department of Health, Education and Welfare (HEW). N.d. 1982 National Long-Term Care Survey: Documentation and Procedures. Washington, D.C.: HEW.

____. 1979. Long-Term Health Care: Minimum Data Set. Washington, D.C.: HEW.

U.S. Department of Housing and Urban Development (HUD). 1987a. Request for submission for additional funds. Washington, D.C.: HUD.

____. 1987b. Memorandum, April 1987. Washington, D.C.: HUD.

____. 1986a. Memorandum, February 27, 1986. Washington, D.C.: HUD.

____. 1986b. Request submission for new funds. Washington, D.C.: HUD.

____. 1983a. Monitoring and Technical Assistance Handbook for the Congregate Housing Services Program (CHSP)--Handbook 4640.1. Washington, D.C.: HUD.

____. 1983b. Request for grant application No. H-12152 fiscal year (FY) 1983 Congregate Housing Services Program. Washington, D.C.: HUD.

____. 1983c. Fifth Annual Report to Congress on The Congregate Housing Services Program. Washington, D.C.: HUD.

____. 1982. Request for grant application No. H-10614. Washington,D.C.: HUD.

____. 1981. Second Annual report to Congress on the Congregate Housing Services Program. Washington, D.C.: HUD.

____. 1980a. News release. Washington, D.C.: HUD.

____. 1980b. Request for grant application No. H-6340. Washington, D.C.: HUD.

____. 1979a. Request for grant application No. H-6200 fiscal year (FY) 1979 Congregate Housing Services Program. Washington, D.C.: HUD.

____. 1979b. HUD News. Washington, D.C.: HUD.

____. 1979c. Request for grant application No. H-6201. Washington, D.C.: HUD.

U.S. General Accounting Office (GAO). 1987. Grant Formulas: A Catalog of Federal Aid to States and Localities, Washington, D.C.: GAO.

Vanhorenback, S. 1986. Congregate Housing: The Federal Program and Examples of State Programs. Washington, D.C.: Congressional Research Service, Housing Economics Division.

Weissert, W. 1985. "Seven Reasons Why It Is So Difficult to Make Community-Based Long-Term Care Cost-Effective." Health Services Research 20(4): 423-33.

Welch, P., V. Parker, and J. Zeisel. 1984. Independence through Interdependence. Boston: Executive Office of Elders Affairs.

Wiener, J., et al. 1987. "Private Long-Term Care Insurance, Cost, Coverage, and Restrictions." The Gerontologist 27(4): 487-93.

Yeatts, D. E., et al. 1987. "Evaluation of Connecticut's Medicaid Community Care Waiver Program." The Gerontologist 27(5): 652-59.

Yordi, C. 1988. Case Management in the Social Health Maintenance Organization Demonstrations. San Francisco: University of California, Institute for Health and Aging.